WITH COMPLIMENTS OF

ATLANTIC
BANK

OF NEW YORK

"Planet Football."

Pete Davies, *All Played Out*, 1990

"There is no mistake about it: the exercise is a passion nowadays and not merely a recreation. . . . It is something else as well as a passion. It is a profession."

The Nineteenth Century, 1892

"The way some people talk about soccer, you'd think the result of one game was a matter of life and death. They don't understand; it is much more than that."

Bill Shankley, former manager, Liverpool Football Club

SOCCER!
THE GAME AND THE WORLD CUP

Forewords by
Joseph S. Blatter
and Alan Rothenberg

Edited by Elio Trifari
and Charles Miers

Design by
Mirko Ilić

Essays by Elio
Trifari, Giuseppe
Castelnovi, Pierfrancesco
Archetti, Fabio Licari,
Sergio di Cesare, and
Alberto Cerruti

RIZZOLI
NEW YORK

in association with
World Cup USA 1994
and

La Gazzetta dello Sport

WorldCup
USA94™

© 1991 WC '94 TM

WORLD CUP USA 1994 BOOK OF SOCCER

First published in the United States by Rizzoli International Publications, Inc.
© 1994 Rizzoli International Publications/La Gazzetta dello Sport
and World Cup USA 1994, Inc.

Principal photography provided by:
RICHIARDI; ALLSPORT/GRAZIA NERI; OLYMPIA;
Farabolafoto, Bob Thomas/Richiardi; Tony Quinn, John McDermott, Jerry Liebman,
La Gazzetta dello Sport. All photographs © the photographers and agencies as listed.
Credits accompany photographs, except as below. The publisher has made every effort
to identify copyright holders of materials in this book. Any omission or exclusion is
regretted and can be included in future printings.

Essays: Africa—Sergio di Cesare; Fans—Pierfrancesco Archetti and Fabio Licari;
Maradona—Fabio Licari; Pelé—Pierfrancesco Archetti; Team USA—Alberto Cerruti;
Women Players—Giuseppe Castelnovi and Jen Bilik

Front cover: Roberto Baggio (David Cannon, Allsport/Grazia Neri); Diego Maradona
(Olympia); Marco Van Basten (Richiardi); Karl-Heinz Riedle (Tony Quinn); Back cover:
Pier Luigi Casiraghi (Richiardi); Francois Omam Biyik (Neal Simpson, Empics, Bob
Thomas/Richiardi); Endpapers: Stadio Centenario, 1930 World Cup venue (Olympia).

Pages 2–3: The Silverdome's (Pontiac, Michigan) artificial surface was replaced with
California-grown grass in July 1993 for the first FIFA-sanctioned indoor soccer game,
England vs. Germany. 2,000 large hexagonal metal trays held the grass over the
winter to replace the artificial surface again for the 1994 World Cup (David Cannon,
Allsport/Grazia Neri); Pages 4–7: Jürgen Klinsmann (Germany and Monaco) scores in
Germany's 2–1 victory over England in 1993 U.S. Cup (David Cannon, Allsport/Grazia
Neri); Pages 8–9: Germany's Jürgen Klinsmann, Italia 1990 second-round 1–0 victory vs.
Netherlands (Richiardi); Page 11: Colombia's forward Faustino Asprilla is widely tipped
as one of the great emerging stars to come from South America. He has played in Italy
for Parma since 1992 (Richiardi); Pages 12–13: Goalkeeper Florian Prunea (Romania and
Dinamo Bucharest) storms over his defender in 2–1 victory vs. Wales, final World Cup
qualifying tie, November 17, 1993 (Chris Cole, Allsport/Grazia Neri); Contents:
Marseilles vs. Lech Poznan, European Cup, 1990 (Fablet, Sipa/Olympia); Holland's Dennis
Bergkamp vs. Denmark's Erich Larsen, 1992 European Championships (Christian Liewig,
Temp Sport/Richiardi); Page 17: Chris Henderson (Team USA) and Cafu (Brazil and
São Paulo) clash in Brazil's 2–0 victory in New Haven in U.S. Cup 1993 (D. Strohmeyer,
Allsport/Grazia Neri); Pages 18–19: A.C. Milan, Europe's most successful professional
club team in the 1990s, at "Milanello," their training camp, 1992 (Richiardi); Pages 20–21:
German boys at the 1988 European Championships in Cologne, Germany. FIFA estimates
that 120 million children participate in organized youth competitions (John McDermott).

Library of Congress Cataloging-in-Publication Data

Soccer! : the game and the World Cup / in association with World Cup USA and
La Gazzetta dello sport ; edited by Charles Miers and Elio Trifari ; foreword by Joseph S.
Blatter ; preface by Alan Rothenberg. p.   cm.
ISBN 0-8478-1806-3
1. World Cup (Soccer). 2. World Cup (Soccer)—History. 1. World Cup USA.
11. La Gazzetta dello sport.
GV943.49.S69   1994   93-46933
796.334'668—dc20   CIP

Additional photo credits:

PP. 4–7, DAVID CANNON, ALLSPORT/GRAZIA NERI; P. 11, RICHIARDI; PP. 12–13, CHRIS COLE, ALLSPORT/GRAZIA NERI; PP. 22–23, SIMON
BRUTY, ALLSPORT/GRAZIA NERI; PP. 34–35, G. PASQUINI, OLYMPIA; PP. 46–47, PP. 82–83, PP. 94–95, SIMON BRUTY, ALLSPORT/GRAZIA
NERI; PP. 86–87, OLYMPIA; P. 96, STEVE POWELL, ALLSPORT/GRAZIA NERI; PP. 104–105, WALTER SCHMITZ/BILDERBERG/GRAZIA NERI;
PP. 112–113, PP. 126–127, PP. 156–157, SHAUN BOTTERILL, ALLSPORT/GRAZIA NERI; P. 117, DEWILDENBERG, SYGMA/GRAZIA NERI;
P. 120, RICHIARDI; P. 121, MAGNI, RICHIARDI; PP. 130–131, PP. 166–167, BILLY STICKLAND, ALLSPORT/GRAZIA NERI; PP. 136–137, BOB
THOMAS/RICHIARDI; P. 161, TONY DUFFY, ALLSPORT/GRAZIA NERI; P. 162, TONY QUINN; PP. 164–165, GILBERT IUNDT, TEMP
SPORT/RICHIARDI; PP. 166–167, BILLY STICKLAND, ALLSPORT/GRAZIA NERI

Printed in the United States of America

Editors' Note

This book, like the 1994 World Cup, would not have been possible without the cooperation of an international team of writers, photographers, photo researchers, editors, administrators, and soccer professionals working toward a common goal: presenting the world of soccer in its finest and fullest light to America.

This vision was shared by the staffs of *La Gazzetta dello Sport* in Milan, Rizzoli International Publications in New York, and World Cup USA 1994, who converted their enthusiasm for soccer into a mission to make this publication as definitive and current as possible.

We were most assisted in this enterprise by the extraordinary goodwill and knowledge of Tony Hicks, Tony Graham, and Lee Martin of the Allsport photo agency and their counterparts at Grazia Neri in Milan; and of Maria Nopanen, Elena Motetti, and Franco Richiardi of Richiardi photo agency in Milan. They provided us with images up to and including the critical confrontations of November 17, 1993, when the last qualifiers for World Cup USA were determined.

Thanks also are due to Cesare Galimberti and Maurizio Scotti at Olympia and to Livio Caffi at Farabola photo agencies in Milan, and to photographers John McDermott, Jerry Liebman, and Tony Quinn, all of whom generously shared their work with us. In England, Graham Smith, collector, Graham Hughes of Wolverhampton Wanderers, and David Bloomfield of the Football Association were extremely helpful.

At *La Gazzetta dello Sport*, Europe's leading daily sports publication, Franco Rubis perceptively opened the doors to incomparable archives of current and historic photography. Giuseppe Castelnovi and Sergio di Cesare assisted in incomparable ways. Pierfrancesco Archetti and Fabio Licari are to be praised for their thorough research and writing. At FIFA, Guido Tognoni, head of the press department, was generous with his time and assistance.

At Rizzoli, Antonio Polito, who shared our vision and our passion for soccer from start to finish, Gianni D'Angelo, and Judith Joseph made the book possible. Thanks also are due to the dedication of Jen Bilik, Andrea Brown, Amelia Costigan, John Deyling, Cathryn Drake, Chris Fodor, Sherrie Murphy, Sam Reep, Michael Shatzkin, James Schulman, Dan Tucker, Steve Sears and, especially, Luigi Bergomi and Elizabeth White.

At World Cup USA, we are greatly indebted to Jim Trecker, senior vice president and press officer, and to Jeff Bliss, senior vice president for marketing, both of whom offered incomparable support for this publication. We also could not have done this project without the advice and assistance of John Griffin, Richard Levine, Jill Labert, Ric Fonseca, and Susan Stimart. Our very special thanks, as well, to Fiona McCormack.

Insofar as Gary Lineker, England's former captain, is correct in saying that the players provide the poetry and the commentators provide the prose, we owe our final thanks to Mirko Ilić, the designer of this book, for making the prose attractive and the poetry special.

Elio Trifari
Charles Miers

Contents

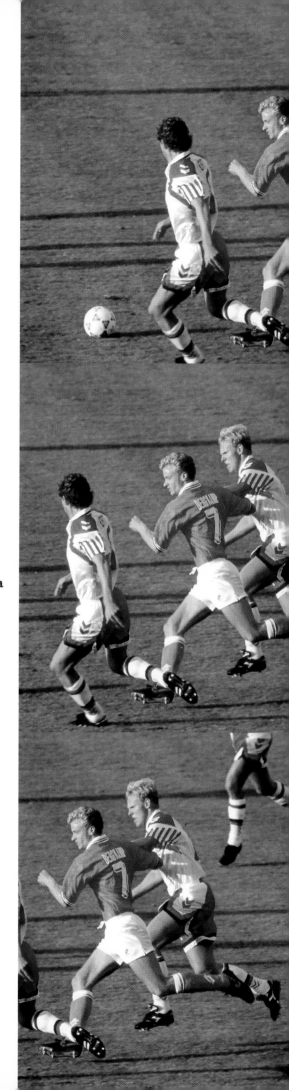

"The World Cup is simply the biggest
sports happening in the universe. . . . Get ready."

The New York Times, **November 29, 1993**

International Football

Nineteen ninety-four promises to be a special year for football and for FIFA. Of course, every World Cup year marks a milestone in the history of our sport, as a new world champion is crowned and the attention of a worldwide audience is concentrated with unparalleled intensity on the four weeks of matches.

But this World Cup year will attract special attention, not only because the number of televiewers is expected to reach an unprecedented 3.2 billion, but because the world's foremost football event is being held in what can almost be described as virgin territory: the United States.

While the last World Cup—four years ago—took place in Italy, one of the world's most traditional football countries, with its long history, established soccer values and achievements, and deep-rooted passion for the game, this year's finals will set out to conquer new ground and to win new enthusiasts.

FIFA has faced this challenge with excitement and confidence, and we are happy to receive whatever support is offered from the established football countries to help us achieve our goals.

In this sense, we particularly welcome this publication from Italy and the United States, safe in the knowledge that the high caliber of journalists and others involved in its compilation have spared no effort to present our sport in all its glory and thus to help achieve the special goals that football, and FIFA, have set for themselves in 1994 and beyond.

Joseph S. Blatter
General Secretary
Fédération Internationale de Football Association

Soccer: An American Vision

"**H**osting the greatest World Cup in history and leaving a legacy for the sport of soccer in the United States." This is the mission statement of World Cup USA 1994, and it is my vision that the World Cup kick-start the sport of soccer by converting the millions of soccer participants in this country into professional league fans and disproving the myth that it is not an American game. Contrary to popular belief, there is a tremendous interest here in soccer, with sixteen million people in the country already playing the game. In a brilliant move, FIFA took the number one sport in the world and the most influential nation in the world and brought them together with the world's greatest single-sport event. The World Cup will be a shot in the arm for soccer in the United States, and FIFA will not be disappointed with its decision. This high-profile event will allow the American people to sample the excitement and passion of this great game.

The future success of pro soccer in the United States will rely on step-by-step development. You cannot successfully challenge the traditional sports overnight. Indeed, soccer is a sport rich in tradition and history, and we must do all we can to help the game find its proper place. A solid foundation must be built. The only element missing is a league—that is where Major League Soccer (MLS) comes in. The mission of Major League Soccer is to join the NHL, NBA, NFL, and Major League Baseball as the fifth major team sport in the United States and to produce players and

teams that are competitive on an international level. The MLS will launch twelve teams in spring 1995.

Unlike other professional sports leagues, which are confederations of independent owners, MLS will own all of the teams initially. A group of corporations or individuals will own the league and hire employees to run each team. This single-entity structure will allow MLS to avoid disparity in the financial stability of team owners, maintain strict financial control, offer a league-wide integrated marketing program, control all major aspects of team operations, and enforce salary caps.

The time has come to promote a more attacking brand of soccer. Thus MLS will consider experimenting with the laws of the game as FIFA requests. We have held a series of brainstorming sessions on possible rule changes that can be implemented to encourage an attacking style of play. The MLS will emphasize aggressive, offensive, highly skilled soccer play while keeping a sensible respect for the established structure of the game.

My vision of soccer comes from an early soccer education. I got my start as general manager of the Los Angeles Wolves of the United Soccer Association and later owned the Los Angeles Aztecs of the North American Soccer League (NASL). As commissioner of soccer for the Los Angeles Olympic Organizing Committee, I was responsible for the soccer tournament, which drew the largest crowds of any sport at the 1984 Olympic Games.

The horizon holds nothing but hope for soccer in the United States for both men and women. I see World Cup USA 1994 as the dawn of a great future.

Alan Rothenberg
Chairman and Chief Executive Officer
World Cup USA 1994

The Soccer World

Above: World Cup 1990, Italy vs. USA from the press box. Right: Soccer in Cameroon, 1993. The plated scoreboard is changed by hand. Racing Club, from Bafousam, won the national title in 1989. Theirs is the country's third largest stadium, holding 35,000 people. Preceding pages: The bare basics in Zambia, 1993. Such handmade balls can last a week.

On a large part of the planet soccer is the way of life. There are an estimated 120 million professional and amateur registered players; fans and spectators can only be measured in the millions per season; roughly a billion people from four to ninety years of age (some even younger or older) practice kicking a ball on sand, on grass, and on hard or muddy playgrounds. Seven of the world's eight most watched sports events have been soccer broadcasts. The 1990 World Cup Final was the world's most watched sports event, beamed live to 1.06 billion people. Five thousand journalists and 2.16 million people attended the tournament. In a decade that is apparently seeing a huge decline in political ideology and spiritual faith, soccer remains both a distinctive passion and a common religion. The noteworthy exception is North America, now that even in Asia, from Japan to China, the game has started to be accepted as a component of daily life.

Signals have been coming from the United States and Canada that soccer is beginning

to penetrate the rituals of young American people, especially in colleges, where women in particular are progressively embracing the sport. Among soccer experts it is indisputable that a revolution is about to start in the United States. If hosting the World Cup finals and starting a new professional league is likely to be a turning point, the shift should be evident within a few months. After the Cosmos adventure started in the mid-1970s we all expected a huge upsurge in the popularity of soccer in North America, but we are still waiting.

When the idea of this book began, we had a fundamental problem to face: to understand who the target audience would be, what level of soccer knowledge was to be expected among American readers, what kind of language we could use (technical, authoritative, highly informed—or the opposite). We have chosen to offer you an informed book, with plenty of facts and history, with quotes and firsthand opinions or memories of leading players, and with statistics and tactics—a comprehensive book for readers who want to learn more about a game they already watch and love.

For our part, we tried to understand why soccer has encountered so much difficulty penetrating the North American way of life. First, it is very difficult to compete with the native games: baseball, football, basketball, and ice hockey. An American citizen tends to take them personally as games made and developed as a part of the American culture. Yet one of these American "national games" was the result of a personal rearrangement of a popular way of playing English football that developed in the early nineteenth century in England: according to tradition, rugby football was started by William Webb Ellis in 1823 when he broke the rule for so-called fair catching and passed the ball with his hands.

Why did one descendent of English rugby, American football, become so popular in the United States, whereas the other—soccer—failed to catch on? Maybe it was the unfamiliar name, derived from one of the many different denominations of the game: Association Football, they called it, then only Association, and then it was corrupted into soccer. It was Charles Wreford Brown, a player for England's Old Carthusians and Corinthians, who coined the word "soccer." The name aside, a derivation of one form of mob football, the so-called hurling at goal, had been imported by the Mayflower-era pilgrims and gained prominence in several colleges during the second half of the nineteenth century, notably at Harvard, Yale, Princeton, and Columbia. Apparently the turning point was Harvard's conversion to rugby football, and then simply to football, which prevented the development of soccer in the United States. Between 1870 and 1880 several colleges adopted Harvard's choice, and soccer disappeared from the campuses.

Looking back to early history, the game started just after the first humans began to transform themselves from pure hunters into peasants and agricultural workers. Leisure time became an element of daily life. Games and hobbies, individual and collective activities, appeared in a society in which until then people had only tried to feed themselves, to seek protection from the elements, and to affirm their superiority over nature. (Yet surely even these early humans also tried to throw and pass stones between one another, and probably most preferred the spherical ones.)

Early accounts of collective ball games exist from Asia to Greece (*episkyros*), and from Rome (*harpastum*) to Egypt, even if the main use of the ball was individual gym exercise—a demonstration of a person's equilibrium and balancing ability. In spite of the fact that such a ball was not rolled on a smooth gym or arena floor, a predecessor to the modern game had begun, and not only in the Mediterranean area. Traces of

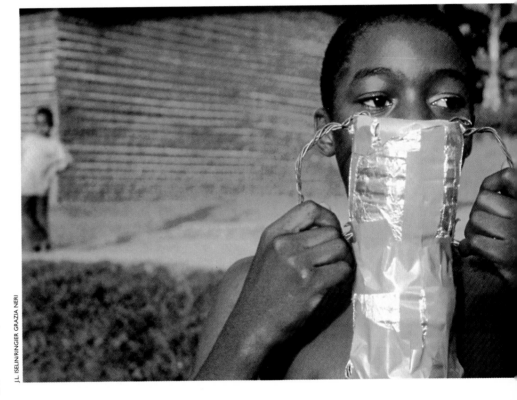

A soccer child in Cameroon.

similar games have been found even earlier: During the second century B.C., the Chinese played *tsu-chu*, literally "kicking the ball with feet," and the Japanese, one millennium later, exercised *kemari*, with eight players on a team trying to kick a ball toward a "goal" delimited by trees.

A recently discovered text recounts a match between Chinese *tsu-chu* and Japanese *kemari* players held in 50 A.D. We might amusingly call this the first international "soccer" match. Other competitions, mainly based on the Roman *harpastum*, were organized between Roman legionnaires and British Isles inhabitants: In 276 A.D. one of these matches, officially documented, was won by the Britons.

The British had clearly developed a specific skill for the game, and it started to spread under the general name "mob football," though there were two variants. The first, called "hurling at goal," was played in small fields by teams of thirty to fifty footballers with the aim being to dribble the leather ball into the opponent's goal. The second, "hurling in the country," was really a bloody battle in the fields between two villages, played on festive occasions, until one group transported the ball into the enemy's central square by almost any means necessary.

Slightly more civilized variations of the game, though still quite rough, were played in the aristocratic schools: There is a reference in the Eton College history from 1519 to boys kicking around "balls full of wynde." Eton developed a football variation called the "field game," which was officially codified in the mid-nineteenth century and included rules that are a cross between rugby and soccer (still played, it has evolved separately from either sport). At about the same time, the "wall game" developed at Eton, in which a ball is bounced off a wall (built in 1717) adjacent to the field, and a door and a tree at either side are used as goals—this is how sports serendipitously evolved. (Interestingly, too, a goal has not been scored in an official wall game since 1909!)

A football phenomenon thrived in Florence in the sixteenth and seventeenth centuries. *Calcio fiorentino* (Florentine football) was another hard battle between two massed teams, each with twenty-seven players. There were a lot of bone fractures and blood—this at the height of the Renaissance. Matches were ritual celebrations—played during royal weddings or on the arrival of important guests—and took place in the marvelous Santa Croce square, which is roughly 100 yards long and 50 wide—about the size of a modern football field.

Players were allowed to use their hands and feet to move the leather ball, inflated with air, similar to the English hurling at goal. Only members of the upper classes were allowed to participate, until the affluent bourgeoisie introduced merchants and bank employees. Rich and colorful costumes, sharp conflicts, many players injured at the end of each game—these were the essential characteristics of this harsh amusement. Indeed, several of these games are in fact the ancient elders of rugby and American football. The more elegant and less brutal soccer was yet to be born in Italy.

The need to avoid brutality and riots between players caused a series of royal edicts in England against mob football and its variants starting from the thirteenth century until 1617, when King James I reinstated the game among those officially ordained. King Charles II was even among the spectators of a 1687 match between the servants of the royal crown and those of the Earl of Albemarle. The earl's team won, the king gave prizes, and the chivalry of sports had begun.

Shakespeare's King Lear defines Oswald with a series of epithets, the worst of them being "football player." Indeed, the game spread in spite of the opposition of the Puritans, but after arriving in the first elite public schools as a recreational activity for boys, it evolved into what it is today.

The public schools fostered the notions of fair play and sportsmanship and thus developed the first precise rules for games.

Children in Northern Ireland.

JOHN McDERMOTT

(Although some claim that when the Duke of Wellington made his famous remark that the Battle of Waterloo was won on the playing fields of Eton, it was not because he admired his officers as strong leaders, but rather as fighters trained well in rough school sports.)

By 1850, there were 60-minute football games, goals without a net or horizontal bar, no authorized goalkeeper (until 1871 no one was allowed to touch the ball with his hands, except for "fair catches"), a vaguely recognizable ball, and only a trace of a modern referee.

In fact, the spirit of those early footballers was pure: The nature of the game was to underline the ability to dribble past the opponent; physical opposition was a capital violation of fair play; even passing the ball was interpreted as an admission of inferiority in the art of dribbling. Real referees were not introduced until 1870, when rules became more integral to the game, and did not become a formal component of the sport until 1889.

Between early and modern soccer there is a flow of continuous evolution similar to that of other sports: Any attempt to compare stars of the 1930s and today's top footballers is a little absurd. The 1930s game was a relatively slow, somewhat confused confrontation between two teams with identical lineups. The modern representation is closer to a highly organized field battle.

The same phenomenon has manifested itself in other team sports, but soccer in the last

Hand-lettered poster in Tirane, Albania, for the 1994 World Cup qualifier vs. Northern Ireland.

thirty years has acquired a great deal of sophistication in the players' physical and psychological preparation and their disposition on the field—making it a very different game from that of the first World Cup.

It is difficult to explain why soccer has gained such a degree of popularity, becoming the most played collective exercise in the world, with 190 countries (including some that cannot even gain a place in the United Nations) affiliated with FIFA, world soccer's governing body.

Simplicity and brevity of rules has been crucial, allowing for interpretation. In its early years soccer showed an unusual adaptability to the various approaches of different countries: an elegant game based essentially on dribbling and individual abilities in the Latin American countries; a strong, rapid game rich with individual confrontation in northern Europe; an initially slow and contemplative game in the Danubian area; and a game with a mix of practical teamwork and exceptional skills in southern Europe.

Still today a Brazilian player has an unusual ability to control the ball, even if he is a defender, while a German player is a strong man with robust skills and an aptitude for the team game. When African players first appeared on the scene they became famous for feline movements as well as for tactical inexperience—"extravagantly talented and totally disorganized," as English writer Pete Davies summarized the stereotype. Today Africa is the strongest emerging force in soccer, as in individual sports such as track and field. Its abundance of talented prospective players makes this continent the real future of the game—a future that is already upon us.

This book tries to capture the beauty of a game that has some moments that are quite foreign to American sports, like the scoreless game. If the essential purpose of soccer is to score a goal, what should a spectator think of those endless minutes when no goal is scored, those 0–0 periods that are so unusual in baseball, football, basketball, and even ice hockey? Soccer has, nevertheless, found during its entire history numerous appraisers of the scoreless game: Some of them have even called it a perfect game, the only possible match between two teams in which critical mistakes have been avoided.

As with other collective sports, the increasing popularity of soccer is attributable to tele-

CIS supporters before an April 1992 match vs. England. Left: A Saudi Arabian on his way to practice.

vision and other technological guidance: better broadcasting accuracy, sophisticated replays, close-ups of players, immediate statistical analyses, and multiple points of view have contributed to a worldwide development that is still growing. Even the quality of stadiums has been improved in the last two decades. In the 1970s, a revolution in stadium construction, now restyled to offer some comfort during the show, replaced soccer fields flanked by poor wooden or metal structures that housed thousands of spectators standing on concrete steps (known as the terraces).

From the perspective of television, however, soccer still cannot offer what broadcasters need to integrate advertising with programming. With no time-outs, soccer provides only brief breaks when the ball goes off the field or a player is injured.

FIFA is seriously considering introducing time-outs in which coaches could confer with athletes, a practice that is presently prohibited. By strict adherence to current rules, in fact, a coach can risk a caution or expulsion if he leaves his sideline position to talk to a player.

People both inside and outside of FIFA estimate that the next ten years will be crucial for the evolution of soccer. If soccer succeeds in conquering North America and Asia, assisted by the U.S. World Cup and a possible 2002 World Cup in Japan, the old Association Football will finally be a truly international game, played all over the world.

While discipline is strictly administered in soccer—brawls among players during a game are rare—the explosion of hooliganism and fan excesses during national and international competitions is currently a primary concern of soccer's governing bodies, and of governments themselves. Particularly prevalent in England, these outbursts have escalated to tragic levels: such terrible accidents as the stampede at Brussels's Heysel stadium during the 1985 European Champions Cup Final, as well as random outbursts of violence at innumerable games, have resulted in increasingly tight security at big events, an issue almost irrelevant to other professional sports.

Sociologists have interpreted these events as the instinctive reactions of underprivileged groups who, marginalized from affluent society, attempt to gain respect and importance through soccer. Most hooligans candidly admit to attending matches only to vent their rage, often not even watching the action on the field.

This phenomenon is not a consequence of soccer itself; rather, it stems from the use of soccer as a medium for expressing frustration at social inequalities. It is nonetheless one of the most urgent problems facing soccer today, and such explosions must somehow be eliminated.

The history of soccer is, in its first decades, a history of rules. No fewer than five meetings were held between the October 26, 1863, founding of the Football Association in England and the publication, on December 8 of the same year, of the set of rules that are the first incarnation of modern soccer. By studying the evolution of soccer through its rules, one can trace the game's progressive movement away from rugby (and, very noticeably, from rules found in American football).

The following rules of the Football Association were adopted on December 8, 1863:

I. The maximum length of the ground shall be 200 yards and the maximum breadth shall be 100 yards. The length and breadth shall be marked off with flags. The goals shall be defined by two upright posts 8 yards apart, without any tape or bar across them.

2. The winner of the toss shall have the choice of goals. The game shall be commenced by a place kick (kicking the ball while it is on the ground, in any position in which the kicker may choose to place it) from the centre of the ground by the side losing the toss. The other side shall not approach within 10 yards of the ball until it is kicked off.

3. After a goal is won, the losing side shall kick off and goals shall be changed.

4. A goal shall be won when the ball passes between the goalposts or over the space between the goalposts (at whatever height) not being thrown, knocked on, or carried.

5. When the ball is in touch (the first part of the field beyond the line of the flags), the first player who touches it shall *throw* it from a point on the boundary line where it left the ground in a direction at right angles with the boundary line, and it shall not be in play until it has touched the ground.

6. When a player has kicked the ball, any one of the same side who is nearer to the opponents' goal line is out of play and may not touch the ball himself nor in any way whatever prevent any other player from doing so until the ball has been played, but no player is out of play when the ball is kicked from behind the goal line.

JOHN MCDERMOTT

7. In the case the ball goes behind the goal line, if a player on the side to whom the goal belongs first touches the ball, one of his side shall be entitled to a *free kick* from the goal line at the point opposite the place where the ball shall be touched. (In the case of a free kick, the opponents shall be positioned at no less than 6 yards from the ball).

If a player of the opposite side first touches the ball, one of his side shall be entitled to a *free kick* (but at the goal only) from a point 15 yards from the goal line opposite the place where the ball is touched; the opposing side shall stand behind their goal line until he has had his kick.

8. If a player makes a *fair catch*, he shall be entitled to a *free kick*, provided he claims it by making a mark with his heel at once; and in order to take such a kick, he may go back as far as he pleases, and no player on the opposite side shall advance beyond his mark until he has kicked.

9. No player shall carry the ball.

10. Neither tripping (throwing an adversary by the use of legs) nor hacking (kicking an

Brother and sister play the simplest game in Milan, Europe's soccer capital.

adversary intentionally) shall be allowed and no player shall use his hands to hold or push an adversary.

11. A player shall not throw the ball nor pass it (i.e. with hands) to another.

12. No player shall take the ball from the ground with his hands while it is in play under any pretence whatever.

13. A player shall be allowed to throw the ball or pass it to another if he made a *fair catch* or catches the ball at the first bounce.

14. No player shall be allowed to wear projecting nails, iron plates, or gutta-percha [a sticky latex sap] on the soles or heels of his boots.

Although these rules are recognizable as the ancestors of modern soccer, many are equally relevant—in some instances, more relevant—to contemporary rugby. Conversely, though none of the original laws today remains unaltered, many of the underlying principles of Association Football have been retained.

Children taking soccer lessons in Cameroon.

From these fourteen rules, it is evident that Association Football derived many principles from rugby. A goal with poles and no bar; play permitted behind the pole; action stopping when a defender touches the ball behind the goal; a score if the ball passes between the poles at any height; the offside rule applying to all players ahead of the one who kicked the ball; the free kick allowed on request to players who touch the ball when it is in the air: all are rugby rules, most of them still valid today.

The "fair catch"—a common event after kickoffs in American football—simply meant intercepting the ball while it was in the air. It is interesting to note that players had to "claim" their free kicks, and that no one "scored" a goal because each goal won a game. The number of games was recorded by the referee, who notched marks on the poles—literally scoring them!

Documents earlier than this 1863 rulebook, however, show that the germination of modern soccer was already present. An 1860 guide by Reverend J.C. Thring, written in order to organize a game for boys at England's Uppingham School, includes rules more contemporary than those of the Football Association's first treatise. In Reverend Thring's "Simplest Game," a score is counted whenever the ball is forced through the goal and under the bar, and playing behind goals was not allowed (rather, a return kick was sanctioned).

The Football Association's code was really quite experimental, modeled after rules in place at Harrow, Eton, and Cambridge colleges, though several of Reverend Thring's points were subsequently adopted. During the Association's early years, alterations were frequent and were followed only by the clubs in or near London. In the north, various Sheffield-area clubs had formed themselves into an association in 1866, adopting a code of laws that differed in many respects from those of the Football Association.

TONY DUFFY, ALLSPORT/GRAZIA NERI

A child in the Brazilian *barrios*, birthplace of the world's most imaginative players, emulates his heroes, Pelé, Socrates, and Rai.

Seven years after the Football Association's first rules were formed, both the London and Sheffield areas exhibited slight but significant differences in play: a crossbar had been introduced between the goal's poles, but the Football Association still used tape while Sheffield had already implemented a wooden bar. After the ball went out of play, the F.A. allowed a hand throw, while Sheffield imposed a kick but had already introduced the premise of this being taken by a player not from the team that had kicked it out.

Regarding the offside rule, the F.A. insisted that all players ahead of the ball were offside, while Sheffield adhered to a curious variant: "Any player between an opponent's goal and goalkeeper is out of play," read the Sheffield rule, "unless he has followed the ball there." This is the first mention of a specific goalkeeper, a transient position that had been assumed by whichever defender stood nearest to his own goal, though Sheffield still prohibited the goalkeeper from using his hands.

The first international match was played on November 30, 1872, between England and Scotland (represented by Glasgow's Queen's Park club). The inauguration of the F.A. Cup precipitated an 1877 merger between F.A. and Sheffield laws. A new and revised set of rules was published in 1878, with some significant steps toward modernization: the goalkeeper could touch the ball with his hands, but could not carry it. Some limitations were still retained: a goal could not be scored from a free kick, a kickoff, or a corner kick, and one player could charge or tackle another player with his back to the opponent's goal.

On December 6, 1882, the International Board was founded, composed of two members each from the English, Scottish, Welsh, and Irish Associations, which adopted the 1878 rules. The International Board has retained the power to set soccer's rules ever since—and in fact FIFA had to apply in 1904 to join the International Board.

Another milestone was reached in 1886 when the International Board published the first memorandum for referees, consisting of a close interpretation of some controversial points.

In 1891 the International Board conducted a major revision of the laws, introducing three new rules and raising the total to the famous seventeen basic rules. Added laws included the definition of the referee and two linesmen's duties; the introduction of a penalty kick for fouls inside the area, defined as the zone within 12 yards from the goal (extending to the touch line); and the installation of a free throw by the referee (which later became a drop kick) to resume play after an interruption.

With rules born, soccer had its constitutional laws and an organization to maintain them. Several national bodies had been formed and England began to tour, sending its first national team to Germany in 1899. Three years later, the first European international match was held in Vienna between Austria and Hungary.

Although it is beyond the scope of this book to trace a detailed evolution of soccer's rules, it is important to point out some significant facts. Today's field dimensions were fixed with rectangular penalty areas in 1902, and an advantage clause was added as a recommendation to referees. In 1903 goals could be scored directly from free kicks.

The characteristics of the ball were defined in 1905, and rules for fair charging were introduced to reflect the actual circumstances in matches. The goalkeeper's use of his hands was progressively restricted, first to his own half and then, in 1913, to within his own area.

In discussions of soccer rules, the majority of debate has centered on the offside rule, which remains a source of controversy. The offside rule was originally derived from the "fair game," when soccer was a matter only of a player's ability to dribble past the adversary to reach the goal. Under this system of play, all players ahead of a team member who had the ball gave themselves an unfair advantage. Restrictions began to rise in response. In 1907 it had already been stated that a player was not offside when he was within his own half of the field at the moment the ball was played by team members. A player was not offside when the ball was kicked off from a goal, on a corner kick, or when the ball had last been played by an opponent. These additions also necessitated a clearly marked center line.

The International Board clarified these rules in the referees' memorandum, stating that an offside player could not put himself "on side" except in certain situations: if an opponent next played the ball, if the player was behind the ball when it was next played, or if the player had three opponents between him and their goal line when the ball was played by a teammate. Three opponents became two in 1925, a change that significantly altered soccer tactics. This is still in effect but for a 1990 recommendation from the referees of Italy's World Cup that players be allowed to fall in line with the next to last opposing player.

Rewritten in 1938, soccer's rules have endured only interpretation, fine-tuning, and special recommendations. Soccer is an evolving game, however, and its increasing television popularity has led to certain alterations that improve "televisability" by speeding up the game, avoiding dead time, and expunging violence from the field—if not from the stands.

With the changes to the offside rule, the International Board introduced red cards to expel a defender who is running free toward the goal, if the defender is the last defender in his way, and limited passes to the goalkeeper, now allowed only from head shots by teammates or for unintentional touches. Until that change, passing to the goalkeeper had become a way of killing time.

Soccer now looks to change its rules to accommodate television advertisements: effective time and time-outs; sudden death in overtime periods; the reintroduction, from soccer's early history, of kick-ins from the touch, with a simultaneous suspension of the offside rule; the abolition of indirect free kicks (actually sanctioned for obstructive playing); and the transformation of all defensive fouls in the penalty area into penalty kicks.

To speed things along, other variations are being studied: short corner kicks from the area rather than from the flag; red cards for charging or tackling from behind and for intentional hand fouls by attacking players; a limit to the total number of yellow cards per team; and closer relationships among the referee and the linesmen.

The future of soccer will depend mostly on the spectacular nature of the game, its ability to promote itself in North America and Asia, and improvements toward transforming it into a fully exploitable television game.

With these factors in mind, World Cup USA 1994 could really be a turning point. As it enters the new millennium, soccer could score its most important goal—a goal to be seen by the entire world.

Claudio Reyna, University of Virginia, symbolizes the future of U.S. soccer. Following pages: *Calcio Fiorentino* **is annually reenacted in Florence.**

On April 6, 1896, when the modern sports movement was launched by the French baron Pierre de Coubertin, who invoked the Olympic myth and inaugurated in Athens the first Olympic Games, soccer (or Association Football, as it was formally called in England) was not yet a popular sport. In fact, the sport does not appear among the scheduled activities of the 1896 Olympics. Indeed, at that time, only English soccer had any history behind it.

It was not until 1855 that the first soccer club was established—the Sheffield Football Club—and the first really significant milestone in the development of modern soccer was not until October 26, 1863: In the Freemasons Tavern in London, thirteen delegates representing ten English and Scottish sporting clubs convened to unify their activities and formally organize the way they played the game loosely described as football. One party wanted to continue with the indiscriminate use of feet and hands that some football players enjoyed and to allow the violent methods inherited from the medieval origins of the sport. Others wished to exclude the use of the hands and to eliminate flagrant violence in the game. Instead of reaching an agreement, the two groups divided: the former eventually founded Rugby Union football (officially begun in 1871), and the latter organized the the Football Association in London. In terms of expressing the advent of modern times, it might be noted that this christening of organized soccer occurred in the same year that the first steam-powered underground railway (with a little less than two miles of track) was built in London.

The football-related activities in mid–nineteenth century Britain were part of the sporting renaissance in Europe that led to the first Olympiad of the modern age. The language and codes of competitive athletics formulated by Baron de Coubertin reflect a utopian and generous liberalism and a chivalrous humanitarianism that theoretically exclude from sport the notions of abuse, injustice, and inequality. "Why have I reestablished the Olympic Games?" he wrote. "To ennoble and strengthen sports, to ensure their independence and endurance, and thus place them in a position to better fulfill the educational role which is incumbent upon them in the modern world." Although such codes of amateurism were certainly supposed to be manifested in the playing of football in England's elite public schools, where the first known rules were developed between 1815 and 1848, it might be an exaggeration to relate the birth of modern soccer unequivocally to such noble ideals.

In 1896 when 245 athletes (all men) from thirteen countries marched under the Olympic flag in Athens, only seven of the countries represented (all European) had some kind of official soccer tournament or national championship. The most organized competition was in England, where the Football Association Challenge Cup, open to all comers, was first contested in 1872. The first winner of the English league championship, a round-robin tournament that started in 1889, was the Preston North End Football Club. The F.A. Cup, a single-elimination or knockout trophy, was established on July 20, 1871, and was first awarded the following year to the Wanderers of London (a team disbanded ten years later), who beat the Royal Engineers of London in the final game, 1–0. The F.A. Cup, which is still open to amateur, semiprofessional, and professional teams (indeed, the prestige attached to success in the cup was in part responsible for the development of professionalism, which was a contentious issue in football circles during the late nineteenth and the early twentieth centuries), is still considered by the English to be one of their most important national institutions. As at Wimbledon, the final match (known colloquially as the Cup Final) is played at the venerated Wembley Stadium and is always presided over by a member of the Royal Family, who awards the trophy to the winning team.

The early soccer competitions were not restricted to England. There has been a cup competition in Scotland since 1874 and a league championship since 1890–1891 (first won by Dumbarton Football Club). A cup competition has existed in Wales since 1878. The Northern Irish cup was established in 1881, and there has been a league championship (first won by Linfield Football Club, still one of the dominant powers of Northern Irish soccer) since 1891. Beyond the United Kingdom there were two other championships in the nineteenth century: in Belgium since 1895 (first won by the still-renowned Standard Liège Football Club); and in Sweden since 1896 (first won by Orgryte), the same year as the Olympic Games in Athens.

After the success of the inaugural Olympic sporting competitions echoed across the globe, the map of world soccer began to expand significantly. By the beginning of the new century three new championships came into existence in Europe: in 1897 Holland and Switzerland began organized football championships, and in 1898 the Italian championship was established. In 1900 Uruguay organized the first South American championship, which was won by the Peñarol Football Club of Montevideo. The organizers of the second Olympic Games, in Paris in 1900, timidly allowed a limited soccer entry, risking a tournament with only three teams: Great Britain, represented by London's Upton Park Football Club (since disbanded), France, and Belgium—with the teams finishing in that order.

Even though soccer's potential popular appeal was still a distant vision, the foundations for its progressive growth were laid. At the turn of the century, especially in the British Isles, soccer attracted players from the higher ranks of society, usually students. Once these young men started their careers in commerce and industry, they promoted the game of soccer beyond their class and beyond national borders.

The History of Soccer

Aztec Sports

The ancestry of soccer can be traced all over the world, not only in the games of ancient China and Japan, but also among the rituals of the Aztecs of Mexico, who played a game with evolutionary affinities to both soccer and cricket. Players wielding stone poles attempted to knock a ball through a small ring, fixed vertically on a wall. While the winners were showered with prizes of money and jewelry, the losing captain met an unattractive fate: His beating heart was removed from his body and offered to the gods.

Wherever English industrialists opened offices, particularly in harbor cities where business directly produced international contacts, the English gathered soccer proselytes. The advent of organized soccer at the end of the nineteenth century in Belgium, Sweden, Holland, Germany, and Italy can be directly attributed to this cosmopolitan interchange.

In Genoa, for example, the most important harbor in the Mediterranean, there was a large English colony whose population was active in the port trade, working in particular with cargo ships used to carry coal. Most of the English residents were managers or employees of maritime companies that had opened agencies in Genoa. Far from their own country, these privileged expatriates focused their leisure time on sports they knew from home. They tried to introduce cricket, but it stirred up little curiosity among the Genoese, who thought it was too elitist.

Consequently, the English exported soccer instead. Having originally founded the Genoa Cricket and Athletic Club in 1893, to which only English subjects were admitted, the club's name was changed by 1896 to the Genoa Cricket and Football Club, and its charter was revised to allow Italian members. James R. Spensley, who was a physician employed by an English shipping company as well as an official of the British government and one of the founders of the scouting movement, was responsible for successfully petitioning the club to implement these changes. (Genoa was the Italian association's first championship winner, in 1898.)

At the turn of the century, Switzerland was the primary Continental outpost of soccer. Large numbers of young people from throughout Europe's upper classes attended Swiss colleges, where they played soccer. Because of the country's prominent commercial role in Europe, the Swiss also had considerable contact with businessmen—and therefore soccer players—throughout Europe. In France, soccer developed in the shadow of rugby; in fact, at the beginning of the century, soccer there was managed not by its own federation but by a polysport organization that favored rugby, which was especially popular in the south of France. Soccer reached Hungary by two routes: via direct trade with England and via Vienna along the River Danube. In Austria, the strong English colony operating in Vienna influenced the youth of the liberal

Lo Sport Illustrato

Anno I - N. 14   30 Ottobre 1913.

1913 Italian championship annual, with team shields.

middle class, who perceived anglophile activities to be fashionable. In Germany, the most industrialized country in Europe, the desire to manufacture independently, including sporting materials, encouraged the growth and business of soccer in Berlin, Munich, Hamburg, and Stuttgart; fittingly, a German-made ball was used in the first championship (won by VfB Leipzig in 1903) rather than one imported from England. The extent of English influence even reached czarist Russia, where in 1887 two Englishmen founded the first soccer club.

Yet the story is more complicated: though soccer spread with British colonialism, English clubs rejected any contact with European teams and officials. This may be attributed in part to the political tensions caused by the Boer War. From 1899 to 1902 Boer settlers clashed with British colonialists in South Africa, particularly over ultimate control of the enormously valuable gold and diamond mines. Many Europeans, whose interests were not linked to those of England, sympathized with the Boer cause, even though their testimonials of solidarity were not backed by substantial aid. This led to mutual aversion and suspicion between England and the rest of Europe that tainted the politics of sport, including soccer, causing problems comparable to those faced by the Olympics in the 1980s. Thus England did not participate in the founding of the sport's governing body, the Fédération Internationale de Football Association (FIFA), on May 21, 1904. FIFA, the umbrella organization for all football associations, was the brainchild of the French Robert Guerin and the Dutch Carl Anton Wilhelm Hirschmann. (The first FIFA office was in Paris, on the Rue Saint Honoré.) In 1906, upon reconsideration, the British associations (England, Scotland, Wales, and Northern Ireland) joined FIFA, only to leave in 1919 as a result of residual political tensions after the First World War. Then, in a series of unparalleled turnabouts, England reentered FIFA in 1924 and left again in 1928 after disagreements over definitions of amateurism: FIFA, despite English objections, allowed semiprofessionals to compete against amateurs. The World Cup, in fact, was not contested by the British teams in its first three editions (1930, 1934, and 1938). Britain rejoined FIFA only in 1946, as the passions of the Second World War subsided. Today FIFA is the ruling body for all professional and almost all amateur soccer, although the four British associa-

Classical Evolution

The Western tradition of football evolved from the ancient Greek *episkyros*, a game played on a lined field in which players used their hands to drive the ball beyond the opponent's boundaries, rather like basketball without a hoop. Feet were used to stop, rather than to propel, the ball. From *episkyros* the Romans derived *harpastum*, a difficult game closer to rugby than to soccer. *Harpastum* was very popular among legionnaires, who imported it to the British Isles, where it would become the ancestor of early mob football.

tions have held extraordinary legislative powers over the rules since the turn of the century.

In 1904, when FIFA was founded, soccer was not unknown in the rest of the world. In South America, for example, well-established organizations had been playing the "strange sport derived from rugby" (as described in 1865 by *The Standard*, a journal published for British expatriates in Buenos Aires). In this city, too, as in the European ports, soccer had arrived with English travelers and merchant shipping agents. The first football club in Argentina was founded in Buenos Aires in 1867. In June of that year, this newly founded club arranged the first soccer match in South America to be reported in a periodical. The return match was scheduled to take place on June 29 on an improvised field in the Palermo district. The teams were recruited by advertisements published in the newspapers. An announcement in *The Standard* notified prospective players: "On Saturday, in the district of Palermo, there will be a football match. We ask everybody who is interested in playing to show up with a white and a red cap so that they can be distinguished during the match. A meeting will be held on the ground to explain the rules of the game."

In 1880 two teachers, the Scot Watson Hutton and the Englishman Isaac Newell, had arrived in Buenos Aires to direct English schools and colleges in Argentina—in the capital city and in Rosario, respectively. History remembers them not as teachers but as great pioneers of soccer. Hutton and Newell founded two schools famous for soccer: Buenos Aires and Rosario, of which the traditional representatives are the clubs Rosario Central, founded in 1889, and Newell's Old Boys, founded in 1905. (In 1993 Newell's Old Boys, still one of Argentina's leading clubs, reopened the doors of soccer to Diego Armando Maradona, after the disastrous Spanish experience of Argentina's *pibe de oro*.)

Brazilians fell in love with soccer later than the Argentines. Charles Miller, who was born of English parents in São Paulo and was educated at the Bannister Court School in England, returned to Brazil in 1894 to dedicate himself to the *bolas* and is considered, for the purposes of the historical record, to have been responsible for introducing soccer into Brazil. The first club, C.R. Flamengo, was formed in 1895. The first known photograph of a soccer match in Brazil is dated 1899; the picture shows black players in action in the center of a sandy site. The game is played against a setting

The scrum in the wall game, a form of football invented and played exclusively at Eton College, England's famed school, since the 1800s.

of rich vegetation and swaying palms. The field is identified as the Bom Retiro ("Good Resort"), on the outskirts of São Paulo.

The end of the nineteenth century through to the First World War can be described as the first period of organized soccer and international play. The rules evolved rapidly in that period. At the time of the Freemasons Tavern meeting some basic rules were defined. Although they now appear to be rather primitive, they have in fact remained the fundamental and universal basis for playing the game. We can recognize some obvious though limited departures: For example, regulation games were played using goals without crossbars (until first tape and then crossbars were legislated twenty years later). Paragraph three of the original rules affirmed, "The goals will be delimited by two vertical posts eight yards distant from each other, without any ribbon or bar across them." The fields were also often much larger than modern pitches. On the other hand, some of the earliest rules are still in effect: The number of players was limited to eleven per team, and the length of each match was to be an hour and a half. The team formations were rather rigid compared with those of today: ahead of the goalkeeper there were two backs, in midfield three halfbacks, and the remaining five players were forwards.

On the international level, there were official reports as early as 1872 of an English team playing a Scottish team. But the first official tournament extended to national all-star teams from outside Great Britain was the 1908 Olympic Games in London. Absent from Athens in 1896, soccer in the following Olympic Games was played

Formation of FIFA

The Fédération Internationale de Football Association (FIFA) was inaugurated in 1904 by Belgium, Denmark, France, Holland, Spain, Sweden, and Switzerland, soon to be joined by Austria, Germany, Italy, and Hungary. England first joined in 1906. FIFA's first official international match was Belgium vs. France on May 1, 1904, though England and Scotland had competed several times since the very first international soccer match in 1872. The first American countries to enter FIFA were Canada, Chile, and Argentina in 1912, followed in 1913 by the United States. Egypt was FIFA's first African participant (1923), and Japan was the first Asian member (1929). Australia, the first Oceanian member, joined in 1963.

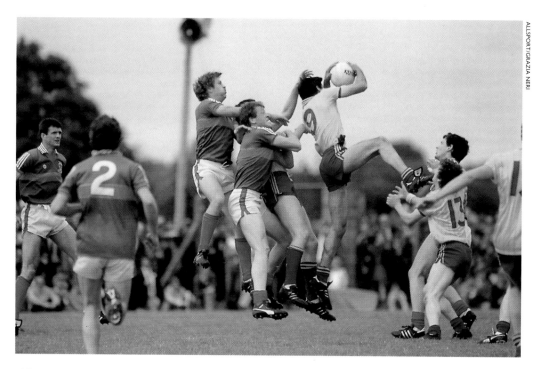

Mayo vs. Roscommon. In Ireland, Gaelic football (seen here) and hurling (played with sticks) are among several traditional sports that share some characteristics with football.

by clubs or hybrid club teams. In the 1900 Games in Paris, the Upton Park Football Club won the gold medal by beating the Union des Sociétés Français des Sports Athlétiques, which represented France, in the final match (4–0). The Canadian team Galt Football Club of Ontario won the soccer tournament of the St. Louis Games (1904), beating the local U.S. team from Christian Brothers college of St. Louis (4–0). Only three teams played at the Paris tournament (English, French, and Belgian sides), and three in St. Louis (one Canadian and two U.S.). Sponsorship for an international tournament was not easy to obtain from the Olympic Committee, which remained dedicated to pure amateurism, even though professionalism was already penetrating soccer in several of the nations that played the sport. But for the London Olympics soccer found an ideal supporter in Daniel Burley Woolfall, an Englishman who was the second president of FIFA.

Five national soccer teams took part in the London Olympic games: Denmark, England, France, Holland, and Sweden. In addition, a second French lineup, called France "B," suffered a resounding defeat in the only match it played, losing to Denmark, 1–17! (ten of the 17 Danish goals were scored by Sophus Nielsen.) The final match was contested by England and Denmark; the Olympic laurel went to the host following its 2–0 victory. The national team championship in the Stockholm Olympic Games of 1912 was also contested only by Europeans, as was that in Antwerp in 1920. The Paris tournament had likewise been competed for by European teams, and the St. Louis tournament (1904) had been

FIFA Presidencies

Robert Guerin's inaugural two-year chairmanship of FIFA was followed by that of Daniel Burley Woolfall, who served from 1906 until his death in 1918. A dispute erupted thereafter between the Amateur Football Association (founded in 1907), the original Football Association (opened to professionals in 1885), and other founding FIFA countries, causing the withdrawal from FIFA of England and the other British associations. Guerin's and Woolfall's presidencies were followed by Jules Rimet (France, 1920–1954); Rodolphe William Seeldrayers (Belgium, 1954–1955), who died less than one year after his installation; Arthur Drewry (England, 1955–1961); and Sir Stanley Rous (England, 1961–1974). Brazilian João Havelange has served since 1974.

an intramural contest between North American teams.

World War I slowed the growth of soccer to paralysis. (Although it is claimed English soldiers challenged Germans to a match on the front lines one Christmas.) World soccer owed its survival through the war to Hirschmann, who kept in contact with the federations affiliated with FIFA from his office in Amsterdam. At the end of the war, following the initiative of the Frenchman Jules Rimet, a future president of FIFA, Hirschmann convened a meeting in Brussels in 1919. The negotiations, however, were difficult because the wounds of war had not healed, and many representatives refused to communicate with each other.

Once the specter of war was removed, soccer thrived. Indeed, in the 1920s the fundamental basis for the success of soccer and for its great popularity were laid. FIFA achieved considerable recognition when, on the eve of the Olympic Games of 1924 (Paris), its proposal to assume the responsibility of organizing an international soccer tournament was accepted. This event marked the turning point for the game: It was now quite rapidly sanctioned, applauded, and valued throughout the world.

Professional players, who had been an increasing part of the game since the 1870s, were allowed to compete in the Olympics through the 1928 Games. In 1932 there was no Olympic soccer tournament; from 1936 professionals were not allowed in the Olympics until the 1970s, when a number of professionals did compete, particularly for Eastern Bloc teams. As a result of the ban on professionals, the Olympics effectively ceased to have an impact on the top tiers of soccer. Currently, any professional under the age of twenty-four is eligible to compete for his national side in the Olympics. In 1924, twenty-two national teams pursued the Olympic gold medal in Paris: Teams from throughout Europe competed, although Britain's soccer players still observed their "splendid isolation." Egypt reached the quarterfinals, giving African soccer its first taste of success. But the greatest surprise was Uruguay. The team revealed to Olympic spectators the wonders of South American soccer, which was previously unknown in Europe: 7–0 vs. Yugoslavia in the first round; 3–0 vs. the United States; 5–1 vs. France in the quarterfinals; 2–1 vs. Holland in the semifinals; 3–0 vs. Switzerland in the championship match, which was played in the Colombes Stadium in front of sixty thousand delighted spectators. On their return to Montevideo, the new Olympic champions were welcomed as the first champions of the world. The success of South American soccer illustrated a style of play different from that of Europe. Individuality and creativity, or "fantasy," were predominant, characterized by elaborate dribbling, feints, precise passing, and quick maneuvers. After seeing the Uruguayan display, which in turn was derived from Argentina, European clubs not only reconsidered their game but felt obliged to compete with the South Americans beyond the Olympic competition.

In the 1920s the rules of the game were definitively codified. In 1925 the basis of the present offside rule was outlined—the rule least easily applied by referees, especially in intense situations when the legality of the position can seem ambiguous. As the only rule in soccer to affect the nature of play and the flow of the game, its implementation—and interpretation—is critical. The rule was stricter before the 1920s. In fact, before 1886, a player could be offside in any part of the ground (no player could find himself more advanced than the ball as it was being played toward the opposing goal—a heritage of the rugby rule). Starting in 1886, a player was considered to be in a legal position if there were at least three other players (including the goalkeeper) between him and the opponent's goal line. In 1907, with the aim to speed up the pace of play, the application of the offside rule was limited: A player could only be offside in the opponent's half. In 1925 a formulation was reached—not much different from today's rules—in which a player had to have at least two opposing players between himself and the opponent's goal line. Today, a player is onside as long as he has at least one opponent in front of him and one level with him. (However, a player in an onside position can run into space behind the defenders as long as the pass precedes him.)

In the 1930s soccer reached a new peak of popularity. The Atlantic Ocean, first traversed via air by Charles Lindbergh in 1929, was no longer an insurmountable obstacle for regular international competition, and not even Black Friday, the great collapse of shares on the New York Stock Exchange on October 24, 1929, and the subsequent global economic depression succeeded in stopping the soccer diaspora. Indeed, the first World Cup, the dream of FIFA president Rimet, opened a new era.

In the 1930s the first myths of the history of soccer were consecrated. They express the game's two schools of thought, the supposed "Latin" style and the English approach. Individualism and the search for the spectacular are considered to prevail in South America, whereas in England, a game emphasizing athletic strength and long passes, deep runs, and aerial confrontations—is expected. Although the English association refused to take part in the first three World Cups, the English team retained an extraordinary aura of invincibility that was not dispelled until the 1950s, when Hungary became the first team to beat England in England. The sense of English dominance in the 1930s was reinforced after the 1934 World Cup, when an English national team beat the Italian World Cup champions.

The effectively symbolic participations of Egypt and the United

Wolverhampton Wanderers Football Club, who beat Everton

States in the World Cup of 1934, and of Cuba and the Dutch Antilles in 1938, revealed the limited progress of soccer in Africa, the Caribbean, and North America. In the United States, where soccer was organized in the 1880s and affiliated with FIFA in 1913, professional soccer was unsuccessful, putting the American game's development well behind Europe's and South America's.

In Europe, the soccer played in the Danube countries was the most admired. The Danubian style of play was best represented by the Austrian national team, coached from 1925 to 1937 by Hugo Meisl, one of the first "magicians" of international soccer. His "Wunderteam" expressed itself through solid defense, precise, short passing and dribbling, a measured and elegant cadence imposed by the midfielders, and the dangerous penetration of the center forward Matthias Sindelar. Following the Austrian example, Czechoslovakia successfully adopted the Danubian methods, so much so that the national team from Prague reached the final match in the 1934 World Cup. Because official competition with English soccer was still not possible and the proponents of the Danubian style wanted to confirm their status as a bona fide

Attendance Records

The largest stadium in the world is Rio de Janeiro's Maracanã, named after the zone in Rio where it was built and accommodating more than 200,000 spectators. Workers took only twenty-two months to construct the arena; it was inaugurated on June 16, 1950, just one month before the famously climactic clash between Uruguay and Brazil in the World Cup Final. Attendance at that game is still the world record for a soccer match: 203,849 ticket holders. The second largest stadium in the world is also in Brazil, the Morumbi stadium of São Paulo, with a capacity of 148,000. The largest stadium in the United States, Pasadena's Rose Bowl, ranks fifth in the world, holding 105,000 people.

1–0 in the 1893 F.A. Cup Final, England's venerable tournament.

war years by Juan "Pepé" Schiaffino, Alcide "Chico" Ghiggia, Dino Da Costa, and Miguel Montuori) could also play on the national side. The significance of this advantage notwithstanding, it was a felicitous time for Italian soccer. Players such as Giuseppe "Peppino" Meazza and Silvio Piola helped Vittorio Pozzo to become the only coach ever to win two World Cups. Pozzo was able to blend the players he selected into an effective side and to unify the country behind the national team.

In the 1930s, however, soccer paid for the broadening of Adolf Hitler's power in Germany. In 1938, after the annexation of Austria, the advanced and feared Wunderteam, which had placed second at the Berlin Olympic Games (1936) and was a semifinalist in the Italian World Cup of 1934, was absorbed into the German soccer ranks because Austria, no longer a country, had to withdraw from the World Cup in France in 1938, where it had been scheduled to meet Sweden in the qualifiers. (Similarly, Yugoslavia also had to withdraw after losing its sovereignty in 1992.)

While the threatening skirmishes of a new world conflict began, soccer still celebrated the sensational success of the Italian teams. Both in 1934 and in 1938 Italy beat Eastern European national teams in the final matches of the World Cup. In 1934 Italy downed Czechoslovakia, whose team included Frantisek Planicka, one of the greatest goalkeepers of any age, and the forward Oldrich Nejedly, the top scorer of the tournament. In 1938 the Italians beat the elegant Hungarian team led by Gyorgyi Sarosi. The "Azzurri" (named after the Italian team's blue shirts) of 1934 were captained by Peppino Meazza, nicknamed *balilla*; the players of 1938 were led by Piola. But it was teamwork that really succeeded.

The national team used a formation, in fashion during those years, called "MM," or "the Method," because of the arrangement of the players: two outside defenders and one halfback (or forward defender), two central midfielders and two wing halfs, and three forwards (see page 166). In the British Isles, by contrast, a scheme called "WM," or "the System," was practiced. The typical British lineup consisted of three defenders, one of whom was in a withdrawn central position (the Method's halfback), four midfielders who formed the "box" (two midfielders and two wing halfs), and three forwards (see page 167). Herbert Chapman, who was appointed the manager (or coach) of the London team Arsenal Football Club in 1925, is historically considered the founder of the System. His tactical scheme foreshadowed a severe man-to-man marking system that found adherents in England but critics in Spain, for example, where the new philosophy of the game was oriented toward zonal play. Chapman's Arsenal won the F.A. Cup and the English league (1930 and 1931, respectively), and the System was almost universally adopted in the postwar period. It was on full view in the World Cup of 1950, which included the English national team for the first time. The formations and tactics now used around the world were derived from this scheme.

The most exciting developments of the 1950s came from the East. Although the Cold War was escalat-

alternative, they launched, as a complement to the World Cup, the Central European Cup for clubs (or Mitropa Cup), in which Austrian, Czechoslovakian, Italian, Yugoslavian, and Hungarian teams took part. Moscow also formally announced a USSR soccer league in 1935, but the national side did not compete outside the huge Soviet borders until later.

In this universe of soccer nations, Italy became a superpower. During the 1930s, to the great satisfaction of Benito Mussolini, whose Fascist party had been in power since 1922, Italian teams won two World Cups and an Olympic gold medal. For the Fascists, as for other dictatorships, success in sports was a propaganda coup. The Fascist government promoted the efforts of Italy's soccer clubs. After the successes of Uruguay in the 1924 and 1928 Olympic Games and the first World Cup (1930), the Fascists combed South America for *oriundi*, foreign-born children of Italian parents, to play for Italian teams. Once in Italy, players such as Luisito Monti (who is the only man to have played for two countries' World Cup teams, having represented Argentina in 1930), Enrico Guaita, Raimundo Orsi (followed in the post-

Championship Cups

The European Champions Cup (now Champions League) and South America's Libertadores (Liberators) Cup determine the continental champions among national club winners. Winner of six trophies in all, Real Madrid has been the most successful club in the Champions Cup, followed by A.C. Milan and Liverpool with four cups, and Bayern Munich with three. Argentina's Independiente of Avellaneda leads in Libertadores Cup victories with six wins. The yearly Super (or Intercontinental) Cup is played between the winners of the two continental cups. The Super Cup, played since 1960, has been won three times each by A.C. Milan and by Uruguay's Peñarol and Nacional teams, both of Montevideo.

First known photograph of a soccer game: Aston Villa vs. West Bromwich Albion, 1887 F.A. Cup Final at the Oval, London. Aston Villa won 2–0.

The Honved team, which was the official Hungarian army side, was allowed to take part in international tournaments. They were abroad when the Soviets invaded Hungary in 1956, and many players very bravely refused to return home. Puskas—who, by virtue of his soccer skills, was made a colonel in the Hungarian army—experienced a period of disqualification and inactivity before ending his career playing for Real Madrid in the Spanish league and for Spain. He was more than 30 years old—quite old by soccer standards of the time—but scored, according to the record books, an extraordinary total of 418 goals.

In Europe in the 1950s soccer was quickly discovered by the pioneers of television, further broadening the sport's borders. Officials of UEFA (the Union of European Football Associations, founded in 1954) realized the potential for promoting soccer on television to a broad European audience, establishing important and exciting knockout trophies for European clubs. The most significant of these have been the European Cup, or Champions Cup (today the Champions League, as it is played on a modified knockout and round-robin basis), the European Cup–Winners Cup, and the Fairs or UEFA Cup. The Champions Cup is contested by teams who have won their country's league championship the previous season. The first dominant power in this competition was the Spanish club Real Madrid, which won the cup five straight times, from 1956 to 1960, while led by Francisco Lopez Gento and Alfredo Di Stefano. The cups were so successful that South Americans used the European model to establish the Libertadores Cup for clubs. At the beginning of the 1960s the new Libertadores Cup was won twice by the Uruguayan team Peñarol. In 1994 the Champions League will be open to more teams from the best European leagues.

In the 1950s and 1960s Brazil also gave its first special present to the history of soccer in the form of the player who is still considered to be the greatest champion of all time: Edson Arantes do Nascimento, or Pelé, as he is known. His Brazil illuminated the soccer firmament, from the World Cup in 1958 to the World Cup in 1970. The number 10 shirt, always donned by Pelé, holds something magical for every player who has worn it since. It is awarded to the most highly rated player of a team—the star, the "image-maker": Bobby Charlton of England in the 1960s (though in the 1966 World Cup he wore number 9); Puskas of Hungary in the 1950s; Johan Cruyff of Holland and Gianni Rivera of Italy in the 1970s; Michel Platini of France and Diego Maradona of Argentina in

ing, Soviet soccer began to compete internationally. The first Soviet soccer ambassador to Europe was not the national team but the Dynamo Moscow team—a club that was able to intimidate established powers (as first discovered by England when the Russian team toured in 1945; the intemperate games provoked outcry from none other than George Orwell, who thought such competitions were poor ways for encouraging international exchange).

From Eastern Europe another important club team, Honved of Budapest, which was the source of players for the Magyar national team, contributed to the game. The technical and tactical innovations of this team included repositioning the center forward, Nandor Hidegkuti, in the midfield, rather than playing him in the traditional center-forward spot. His new role was mainly to assist or feed the remaining two forwards (or wing halfs) rather than taking passes from them. The Method had enjoyed considerable success, and almost every team thereafter played with two outside defenders and a center half, who marked the opponent's center forward, two central midfielders, and two wing halfs behind the three forwards (two wingers and the center forward). But the revolution from Hungary altered the attacking roles: the center forward withdrew behind two inside forwards, who overlapped with the midfielders. He was responsible for drawing the opposing center half out of position, leaving space for the wing halfs, who traveled up with him, to move quickly forward, abandoning the opposition wing halfs in the process. This was so effective that Hungary's Ferenc Puskas became the first inside forward, or number 10, to be the top scorer in soccer.

The Football War

Soccer can supersede or foment international crises, as with the 1969–1970 border disputes between El Salvador and Honduras when, despite fighting, the two countries met on the soccer field to play home-and-home qualifying games amid arguments over the number of El Salvadoran refugees in Honduras. Honduras won the tense first match at home 1–0, but El Salvador scored three goals in the return match to qualify for the World Cup in Mexico, inspiring civic protests and government accusations that led to the interruption of diplomatic relations between the two countries. In the 1982 Spain World Cup qualifiers, the two countries played each other four times, with both countries qualifying.

the 1980s. In terms of team success the 1950s and 1960s were the golden age for the stylish, varied-tempo attack style of Brazil. Indeed, Pelé was not the only Brazilian star. One of the secrets of Brazil's first world triumph in 1958 was the discovery of "Zagalo," Mario Jorge Lobo, who played as a midfield winger in Brazil's 4-3-3 formation. The 4-3-3 formation countered the Italian *catenaccio*, a defensively oriented system of four or five defenders, including a *libero*, or sweeper, that was popular in the 1950s. In 1962, when Brazil defended its world title in Chile, Pelé was injured in the first round. The South American team that year flew with the "young sparrow," Garrincha, the nickname given to Manuel Francisco dos Santos, a winger who was a brilliant player despite having a physical handicap—one of his legs was shorter than the other, yet he was able, like no one else, to make feints that pulled opposing players out of position. After being defeated in England in 1966 by Hungary, Brazil and Pelé returned to win the 1970 World Cup in Mexico.

First known photograph of an international game in Europe. The game was played between a French and an Italian club: Genoa Cricket and Football Club vs. Nice, 1893.

In the 1960s soccer flourished on every continent. Less developed countries in Asia and Africa, now independent of the colonial powers, programmed regular national championships and sometimes employed well-known coaches from Europe or South America whose careers were almost over. The most notable example was "Zagalo", who coached Brazil to its third world title in Mexico before coaching for many years in the Gulf states—in 1990 he coached the United Arab Emirates in the World Cup finals. In 1964 the African club championship was started, first won by Oryx Billois Douala in Cameroon. In 1967 the Asian club championships began; the first team to win was Israel's Hapoel, from Tel Aviv. At the same time, interest in soccer was revived in the United States. A chief proponent was Richard Nixon's statesman, the German-born Henry Kissinger. The first American professional championship was held in 1968 and was won by the Atlanta Chiefs. Professional soccer truly arrived with the advent of the New York Cosmos, a team created in 1970 by two brothers, Nesuhi and Ahmet Ertegun, who had played soccer in their youth in Turkey. The Cosmos became known to the rest of the world after Pelé was signed (for a sum of $4.5 million), followed by such superstars as Jan Neeskens and Franz Beckenbauer. But this brilliant era of American soccer ended in 1982 without really penetrating the country's sports establishment.

The founder of the sport, England, finally won the World Cup at home in 1966 after suffering a humiliation in 1950 (a surprise defeat by the United States and elimination by Spain) and undistinguished performances in 1954 and 1958. Yet perhaps the true revelation of 1966 was Eusebio, a native of Mozambique and prolific goal scorer for the Portuguese team: He was the first African-born player to have an impact on world soccer.

The English world championship team also included players who have become legends—notably the goalkeeper Gordon Banks, the defender Bobby Moore, and, above all, playmaker Charlton, who was gifted with good technique and a clear vision of how to play the game.

The great Brazilian soccer epoch culminated in 1970, with Brazil ruling the tournament in Mexico: The final match with Italy at the Azteca Stadium in Mexico City ended in a peremptory 4–1 victory. The 1970s and early 1980s brought to the fore two styles: "physical" soccer, a fast-paced running game favoring strength and stamina, most exemplified by English teams; and "total soccer," introduced by Dutch teams. Both sides had success: Ajax Amsterdam, Bayern Munich (following the Dutch style), and then England's Liverpool dominated the Champions Cup; the German and Dutch national teams reached the final match of the 1974 World Cup in Munich, and four years later the Dutch team reached the final match in Argentina, but, as in Germany, they were beaten by the host country's team. Soccer in this decade was most influenced by four national team managers: Helmut Schoen of Germany, the Argentine Cesar Luis Menotti, and the Dutch Rinus Michels and Ernst Happel. Holland's national team

FIFA Confederations

FIFA is currently divided into six confederations that host the qualifying rounds of each World Cup tournament: CAF (Africa; founded in 1986), CSF (South America; 1916), CONCACAF (North and Central America; 1961), AFC (Asia; 1954), OFC (Oceania; 1966), and UEFA (Europe; 1954). Israel, which until recently was directly affiliated with FIFA, is now a member of UEFA. Reflecting the tight structure of world soccer, the confederations communicate FIFA's authority to all national associations and leagues. The confederations are responsible for admitting teams into membership, upholding and communicating FIFA's regulations, and representing members at the FIFA Congress.

offered the best example of total soccer: Versatile players were called upon to defend and to attack by sprinting forward or back, to put opposing players in offside positions, to press everywhere, and to continuously change their positions on the field. The new game was exemplified by the Dutch players Wim Surbier and Ruud Krol, defenders on paper who were allowed to advance like wingers. Cruyff was allowed to roam the field, to direct the match from the rear, and to move forward to score goals. The most emblematic figure of the new creed was Neeskens, who was present in every part of the field.

By the 1980s the word "goal" was used on all five continents. Both Europe and South America could boast of stylish and effective soccer, but countries on other continents had begun to make the leap to international caliber. In the 1978 World Cup, Tunisia stopped Germany with a tie (0–0); four years later, in Spain, Cameroon exited the competition due merely to a poorer goal difference than the Italian team (the eventual champions whose team won Italy's third World Cup). The same fate befell Algeria, which was ousted on goal difference by Germany and Austria (after those teams apparently contrived to tie each other in order to advance).

If Cameroon in 1982 seemed no more than the typical overachiever of the league, the 1990 World Cup denied this supposition, confirming the maturity achieved by such players as Roger Milla, Thomas N'Kono, and François Omam-Biyik. After shocking the Argentine national team—the defending champions, led by Maradona—1–0 in the competition's first match, the Cameroon team reached the quarterfinals, to be just edged by England in overtime. But Italia '90 not only blessed the entrance of Cameroon—and Africa—into the soccer pantheon: the undertakings of another national team cannot be overlooked. Colombia, led by Freddy Rincón and René Higuita, one of the most whimsical and eccentric goalkeepers (and therefore—by hook or by crook—one of the most noticed) tied Germany 1–1, which went on to win the cup. The arrival of teams from countries with little soccer history had been suggested at the Olympic Games of Seoul in 1988, where Ghana and Australia played for the bronze medal. The 1992 European Championships and the 1993 World Cup qualifiers have also shown that the field is relatively even at the top strata. An unheralded team from Denmark—a last-minute addition to the competition after Yugoslavia was withdrawn—won the European championships; Norway has reached the finals of the World Cup for the first time since 1938; Bolivia, Switzerland, and Bulgaria have made the finals after achieving stunning upsets in the qualifiers. The United States has also performed well, if erratically, defeating Ireland and England, as well as achieving a tie with Italy, in the past two years.

Soccer in the United States has a long history, and several experiments have been briefly successful (see pages 50–51). While the United States has attempted to gain a foothold in world soccer, a general American lack of interest has led to financial difficulty in almost every soccer endeavor over the last twenty-five years. The North American Soccer League's New York Cosmos was the first team to break into the

Luciano Pavarotti with World Cup stars. Standing, from left: Amarildo, Silvio Piola, Carlos Alberto, Lucien Laurent (the first scorer in the 1930 World Cup), Pavarotti, Gerd Müller,

Fantasies of Soccer

John Huston's 1981 film, *Victory*, was a remake of a Hungarian film, Zoltán Fabri's *Két Félidö a Pokolban* ("Two Times in Hell"). Based on a 1942 match in Kiev between Nazis and Ukrainian prisoners, the Hungarian film stages the game in Hungary in 1944, whereas Huston's story pits Germans against Allied Forces prisoners. An escape is planned during the match as the Allies recover from 1–4 down to tie the game at 4–4. A German penalty kick is saved, in the end, by goalkeeper Sylvester Stallone. A slow-motion bicycle kick by Pelé is a masterpiece of cinematography and soccer. Other players appearing in the film are Bobby Moore, Kazimierz Deyna, and Osvaldo Ardiles.

international scene when they signed Pelé in 1975, but folded with a loss of $52 million in 1985, one year after the league itself had disbanded. Some ideas to alter the game in order to attract audiences have even taken hold. Indoor soccer is an almost uniquely North American phenomenon, a game played according to altered rules that include play continuing after the ball has ricocheted against the walls surrounding the small field. The first indoor league opened with full-size fields and eleven-a-side teams in Boston's Commonwealth Armory in 1923. The Major Indoor Soccer League (MISL) was founded by Earl Foreman, who became its first commissioner, and Ed Tepper in 1978. MISL began with six teams: Though the number of teams (six to fourteen) in the league remained almost constant, thirty-two cities entered teams over the course of the league's fourteen-year lifespan. MISL peaked in its 1985–1986 season when the average attendance at games was up to nine thousand. The league's best team was the San Diego Sockers. After MISL concluded its operations in 1992, two indoor

Felice Borel (played for Italy in 1934), Bobby Charlton, Pepe Schiaffino. Kneeling: Maradona, Paolo Rossi, Pelé, Daniel Passarella (Argentine captain in 1978).

Palestine in October 1993. This visit had important sociopolitical ramifications because it opened the doors of soccer to the new entity. Soccer, however, is a sport with infectious appeal, and its borders have broadened without political revolutions. The latest news comes from a highly developed country: Japan. Since 1980 the Japanese have been hosting the international challenge match between the European Champions Cup winners and the South American Libertadores Cup winners. In 1993 the Japanese had their first intramural championship, attracting a number of international veterans to their league, including England's Gary Lineker, one of the world's most prolific goal scorers. The Japanese national team was excluded from USA 1994, due only to a goal scored by the Iraqi national team in the very last minute of the final qualification match.

At the professional club level there have also been significant changes. Europe's top leagues now attract great numbers of foreign players from other European countries, as well as from Africa and the Americas. Serie A, the top division of the Italian league, has eclipsed the English league as the world's most popular club championship, in large part because of the foreign players. Italian regulations require all clubs to be operated on a nonprofit basis, so there are considerable funds available for reinvestment in players. Serie A teams (A.C. Milan, Juventus, and Parma) won all three European club trophies in 1993.

FIFA has respected and fostered internal and external changes to soccer. A larger multicontinental presence has been granted in the final phase of the World Cup; on the occasion of USA 1994, there will be three African teams, not two as before. In addition to Cameroon, Nigeria will make its debut in the World Cup, a harbinger of things to come from the subcontinent. Greece is Europe's newest arrival, competing in its first finals, and Australia reached the play-off match with Argentina, losing only 0–1 on an own goal in Buenos Aires. Colombia and Mexico promise a new balance of power in the Americas. FIFA has also revamped some paragraphs of the regulations, changing fifty years of tradition in order to speed up play. The back pass by a defender to the goalkeeper is now prohibited. This variant forbids the goalkeeper to seize the ball with his hands if the pass is not a header or from a throw-in. Also, the offside law has been refined: If the attacking player is parallel with the last but one opposing defender, he is not considered to be in an offside position. A highly controversial rule change has been the gradual introduction of the penalty shoot-out to settle games in knockout tournaments that end in a tie after overtime—rather than offering the teams a replay. In the 1990 World Cup, both semifinals ended in this manner, with Italy and England being eliminated. The rule is now being introduced at club level, with England's venerable F.A. Cup, a competition often highlighted by numerous replays, to implement it soon. Sudden-death rules in overtime will be introduced after the 1994 World Cup, and in the 1994 tournament itself attacking football will be rewarded by giving three points, rather than two, for a win in the first round.

And now, finally, the world is to watch soccer in America.

leagues remained: The Continental Indoor Soccer League (CISL) and the National Professional Soccer League (NPSL).

In the last decade, the world has been shaken by events that have changed the political map and consequently influenced international sports. The demolition of the Berlin Wall has strengthened Germany and greatly weakened the former Soviet teams. Teams from Russia, Lithuania, the Ukraine, and Estonia now compete. The Gulf War, the civil war in what was Yugoslavia, the accord between the Jews and Palestinians—all these events are directly affecting soccer. Yugoslavia is no longer allowed to field a team, and Czechoslovakia will become two teams after 1994. Because of the politics of the Gulf War, the final qualification matches between Saudi Arabia, Iraq, and Iran for the 1994 World Cup were followed closely by the media, helping to gain great attention for Asian soccer. And the direct intervention of Saddam Hussein and his son in team selection was widely reported. A delegation of soccer players from France, coached by Platini, toured

Tragedies of Flight

Three major air disasters have struck the soccer world, profoundly affecting the sport. In 1949 an airplane carrying the Torino team crashed, killing 22 members. Torino played out the season with reserves and was awarded, ex officio, the Italian Serie A title. In 1958 an aviation disaster killed most of Manchester United's team; surviving players included England forward Bobby Charlton and the coach, Sir Matt Busby, who went on to win the 1968 European Cup. In 1993, the Zambian national team's plane crashed. Reserves and youth team members played in the World Cup qualifiers, missing the 1994 finals only after losing to Morocco in the last game. *Following pages:* **Zambian National Stadium Memorial.**

The king maintains a secret—only one. Where does it come from, that two-syllable name, Pelé, that dwells in the mythology of soccer? There are two theories to explain the origins of his title: *Pelada,* which in Portuguese is easily reduced to Pelé, is a small, bare field, perhaps one near the house where the wren who was called "Dico" by his family spent the days of his youth; or is it a name that stems from the desire to emulate Quelé, the phenomenal soccer idol of his youth. The rest of Pelé's story is a book missing the final chapter, because immortals have the luxury of infinite history. Edson Arantes do Nascimento has charmed successive generations; he has exhausted thousands of metaphors. They wrote about him, "If he hadn't been born a man, he would have been born a ball." And, "Pelé is to soccer what Shakespeare is to English literature." And still, "Conductor, orchestra, and music: here is what he has been."

His family is a traditional one: His father, Dondinho, was once a reasonably good center forward for Fluminense who was stopped by a fractured leg. He dreamed that his son would also be a soccer player. His mother, Celeste, still today is not ashamed to take care of his needs and would have been happy for him to have completed a scholastic diploma—a story without a future, because the little one had boundless talent for a game.

One day, from Três Corações, where he was born on October 23, 1940, he made his way to Santos. He was 15 years old. On his journey, he made stops at Baquinho and Sete Setembro, amateur teams, and then at Bauru Athletic Club, where the eye of an ex–national team player, Waldemar de Brito, wouldn't let the thin youth get away. Brito recommended him to the Santos.

The predestined often present themselves unambiguously. Before turning 16, Pelé first appeared for Santos against the Corinthians F.C. and scored a goal right away. Ten months later, on July 7, 1957, he had his first encounter with the *Seleçao,* the national team: Argentina won that game in Rio, 2–1, but Pelé scored a goal, and Brazil realized that they had found a treasure.

The world discovered him in Sweden at the 1958 World Cup; he wasn't yet 18 when he won his first Jules Rimet Trophy. Two more followed, in 1962 and 1970, an unprecedented record for a player. He was baptized with new names: O'Rey (the king) and the Black Pearl. After the triumphant start, the trophy room was filled quickly. With Santos he won the São Paulo (Paulist) championships, four cups in Brazil, two Libertadores Cups, and two Intercontinental Cups. He played 112 games (not all of them were official, as FIFA does not count the games played against clubs), scoring 95 goals.

His infectious enthusiasm for playmaking was as contagious as his love of goal scoring. He defined the role of the assist man—the midfielder or inside forward who conducts the attack—and simultaneously he scored at will. He played alongside—or, rather, led—some of the greatest Brazilian players, but even in their company he was unique.

A former teammate has described him as follows: "He has the sudden movement of a center forward, the dribbling of an acrobat; he has the shot, the fake, the pass, the header, the physical resistance. Does he need anything else?" At the summit of his career, he also always had the goal. For ten years in a row he was the "gunner" (the leading scorer) of the Paulist championships. In 1959 he established the season record of 126 goals. On November 21, 1964, he scored 8 goals in a game against Botafogo. On November 19, 1969, with commonplace nonchalance, he surpassed 1,000 career goals. The final sum was 1,284 goals in 1,363 games, a game average of 0.94. There was only one player who ever exceeded him: his fellow countryman, the Brazilian Arthur Friedereich, called "The Tiger," arrived at 1,329 between 1912 and 1937.

Thousands of goals and thousands of anecdotes. And a great deal of facts—not legends. When he left the national team on July 18, 1971, 200,000 people at the Maracanã cried and shouted. Pelé gave his shirt with the number 10 to a ten-year-old boy.

His teammates said that he would have been the best in any position. Once he even insisted on playing goalkeeper. Santos couldn't refuse. He closed the game unbeaten and even averted a penalty. After a trip to Lima, a simple inscription was placed on a wall of the stadium: "Here played Pelé." Pure admiration.

In Nigeria he stopped a war: An armistice of 48 hours was signed with Biafra to allow soldiers and insurgents to attend one of his exhibitions. He never left Santos, with which he ended his career in 1974, although he started again in North America with the New York Cosmos, persuaded by Henry Kissinger, and became an ambassador for soccer in the United States.

On October 1, 1977, he retired definitively after capturing the North American title. He became a businessman after having been an actor and a writer for fun. Today his earnings are approximately $30 million per year. (He has re-emerged from two earlier financial disasters.) He divides his time between a house in Copacabana, a Manhattan apartment, a Long Island vacation villa, and his longtime home in Guarujá along the beach near Santos. His family has recently grown larger with the birth of a son, who joins Rachele, Edinho, and Jennifer. He has announced that he is settling down with a 35-year-old Brazilian psychologist. At 53, he lives brilliantly with his popularity. "I have not tired of being considered a myth," he recently admitted. Certainly the soccer world will never tire of always making him comfortable.

Edson Arantes do Nascimento "Pelé"

Left: Pelé in the uniform of his first club, Santos (for whom he played from 1956 to 1974), at his professional farewell match, Cosmos vs. Santos, October 1977. Pelé played one half for each team.
Below: Cosmos scoreboard in 1977.

JERRY LIEBMAN

s soccer now reaching mainstream America? The Soccer Industry Council of America cites two recently conducted surveys: NCAA and NAIA statistics reveal that whereas 546 colleges have football teams, 581 have men's soccer teams. Among youths, the percentages are still more impressive: Soccer ranks second among boys under 12, with 6.8 million participants, second only to basketball (8.9 million), followed by softball (5 million), touch football (4.9 million), and volleyball (4.6 million). Further proof that soccer is gaining acceptance can be found at the under-18 level, where it ranks third among other sports: basketball (20.5 million participants), volleyball (12.5 million), soccer (11.6 million), touch football (11.3 million), softball (11.1 million), and baseball (9.6 million). The number of soccer players under 12 suggests that the game may make even more gains in popularity as these young athletes grow up.

The history of American soccer began in 1862, when Gerritt Miller Smith founded the first American club, the Boston Oneidas. The Oneidas were undefeated until 1865, playing their games in the Boston Commons, which today has a commemorative plaque to the team. The first intercollegiate match pitted Princeton against Rutgers on November 6, 1876, in New Brunswick, playing by the rules of the newly founded Intercollegiate Football Association. It is unclear whether this was closer to "American" football or soccer—or perhaps a hybrid. The first national league began when a group of clubs from the East Coast created the American Football Association in Newark, New Jersey. Newark was home to the first international match in the United States, when the so-called national team held two games against Canada in 1885 and 1886, losing the first (0–1) and winning the second (3–2). It was not until August 15, 1913, that the United States Football Association (USFA, later to become USSFA and now USSF) was granted a provisional membership in FIFA, gaining full member status the following year. In celebration, a U.S. national team played in Norway and Sweden, becoming the first American side to travel to Europe. Its international debut took place in Stockholm on August 20, 1916, won by the visiting team 3–2 . Three years later, due in part to the success of that first game, the Bethlehem Steel club was invited to Sweden as the first professional American team to tour Europe.

When the American Professional Soccer League (APSL), the first professional league, was formed in 1921, only seven teams were granted franchises: Philadelphia's Fall River, Jersey City's Celtics, Brooklyn's Todd Shipyard, New York's F.C., Holyoke's Falco F.C., and Pawtucket's J.P. Coats. By 1934, one year after the NCAA published the first official rule book for all intercollegiate soccer in the United States, the APSL began to recognize title winners (the first title went to the Kearny Irish team) after a thorough organizational restructuring. The APSL disbanded in 1980, but since World War II it had devolved into a semiprofessional circuit.

In 1967 two rival leagues (NPSL and USSA) merged to form the North American Soccer League (NASL), the most successful soccer league in the United States to date. Begun as a minor team in 1971 and an upset winner of the NASL title in 1972, the New York Cosmos catapulted the league from relative obscurity when, on April 1, 1975, it signed Pelé. He had retired from the Brazilian national team in 1971 and joined the Cosmos for $4.5 million and a three-year contract. In 1976 a forward on the Italian national team (though born in Wales), Giorgio Chinaglia, left Lazio to join the Cosmos. The team won five titles from 1977 to 1982 and was by then drawing such crowds that it had to move its games from Randall's Island to Yankee Stadium and then to the NFL Giants Stadium.

The Cosmos had been the brainchild of an English journalist, Clive Toye, who solicited money from the Warner music and publishing group, run by two Turkish brothers, Nesuhi and Ahmet Ertegun. Millionaire Lamar Hunt and statesman Henry Kissinger had been among the directors of the drive to bring Pelé to the Cosmos and later supported efforts to sign Chinaglia, Franz Beckenbauer, Carlos Alberto Torres, Ruud Krol, and Jan Neeskens. As the Cosmos toured the world, other European players late in their careers were attracted to the NASL clubs. The NASL experimented with changing some basic rules, but was eventually asked to stop by FIFA. With no other choice, the Americans again began playing by international rules, but spectators were disoriented and attendance dropped off. Profits from television rights plummeted, and the Cosmos adventure ended with a loss of about $52 million.

After the Cosmos's downfall, organizers were reluctant to form another professional league in the United States, and American league soccer slowed almost to a halt. A semiprofessional league, the American Professional Soccer League, began in the mid-1980s and now comprises nine teams. A proposed new league, Major League Professional Soccer, is now being organized as part of the plans for the 1994 World Cup.

Soccer in the United States

Giorgio Chinaglia was with Cosmos from 1976 to 1982.

Ricky Davis, star American-born defender for Cosmos.

Franz Beckenbauer, former captain of Bayern Munich and West Germany, played for the Cosmos from 1977 to 1980, and in 1983.

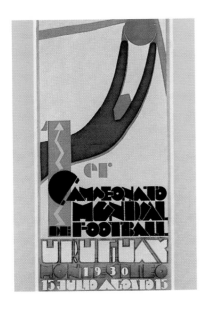

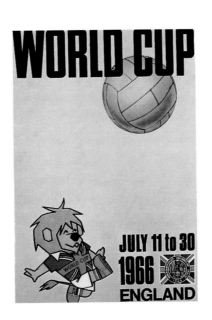

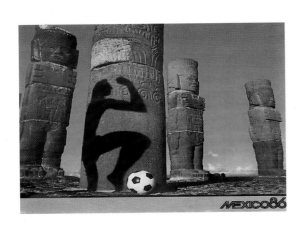

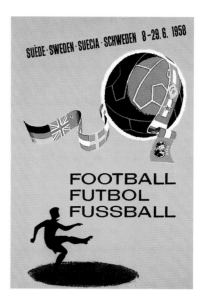

1930 1994

The World Cup

1930
Uruguay

The dream comes true. Uruguay was selected, in the country's centenary anniversary of its independence, to organize the first World Cup. Brazil, Argentina, Chile, Bolivia, Peru, Paraguay, Mexico, and the United States enthusiastically committed teams to the enterprise. European federation reactions, colored by the politics of not being selected as hosts, were disappointingly halfhearted: only France, Romania, Yugoslavia, and Belgium entered—and then only under pressure. The most outstanding European teams were missing—those from Switzerland, Austria, and Czechoslovakia. The British teams were not there either, having battled with FIFA over definitions of amateurism. Italy did not even justify its absence, sparking a controversy with the Uruguayan Soccer Federation and retaliation at the next tournament, in 1934.

Nevertheless, "Mundial fever" overtook Montevideo. A new venue, the Estadio Centenario, was commissioned and built in five months, with workshifts going round the clock. The stadium was readied only on the day of the first match. Uruguay was the bettors' favorite, with low odds also given to Argentina and Brazil. Because of the lack of teams entered, the competitors were organized into four groups, who played on a round-robin basis to produce the semifinalists—and to give spectators enough matches to watch. The first kickoff was on July 13, at 2 P.M., an honor given to the teams of France and Mexico, but in those days of limited international travel, the two sides attracted only five hundred people to the historic occasion.

The first match to instill great expectations was between Uruguay's neighbor, Argentina, and France. The Blue-and-Whites, Olympic silver medalists behind Uruguay in 1928, were confident about their chances. They defied the stereotype that Latin footballers were lavishly skilled but incapable of dedicated training. Carlos Peucelle, one of the Argentine stars, has recalled those days: "Luisito Monti and I ran twenty laps of the field every morning; I had never done this before."

France lost the match amid fierce controversy. After 86 minutes the French player Maschinot found himself with the ball in front of the goal: He seemed certain to tie the score, but the Brazilian referee, Almeida Rego, blew his whistle to signal the end of the game. Then, as now, the referee was the official timekeeper. The game was restarted after some argument, but the French had lost their chance.

The home team made its debut against Peru, before an audience of eighty thousand. The whole country was interested in the team selection, especially as the renowned goalkeeper Supicci paid the consequences of a night on the town before the game and was replaced by

Argentine goalkeeper Angel Bossio's busy afternoon in the Estadio Centenario. Uruguay vs. Argentina, 1930 World Cup Final.

Sailing the Cup

En route to the 1930 World Cup, an Italian ship, the *Conte Verde,* carried not only several European teams, FIFA president Jules Rimet, and FIFA delegates, but also, in the ship's safe, the World Cup itself, made of four pounds of gold by the French jeweler Abel Lafleur. The Jules Rimet Trophy was officially retired to Brazil in 1970, when that team won it for the third time. The present trophy is called the FIFA World Cup. French, Romanian, and Belgian players shared limited deck space to practice among companion travelers, who reveled in counting the many balls that plunged daily into the sea. Also traveling on the ship was the great Russian tenor Chalyapin, who, when asked to sing in commemoration as they crossed the equator, haughtily replied, "Never done gratis."

Enrique Ballesteros. Nevertheless, Uruguay won. At the same time, Argentina was suffering within its group and was almost forced into a play-off with Chile for first place. Forward Guillermo Stabile, however, got his team out of trouble and became the tournament's top scorer.

The semifinal draw favored the promoters: Argentina was to play the United States and Uruguay was to play Yugoslavia. The scent of a replay of the 1928 Olympic final electrified both games. As scripted, Uruguay and Argentina went through to the final. The United States and Yugoslavia

were both hammered by 6–1 scores. Dozens of steamboats brought twenty thousand Argentine fans across the River Plate to Montevideo for the showdown.

The pressure built among the players. Pelegrin Anselmo of Uruguay withdrew without explanation. There were rumors that he was scared of Monti's ruthlessness, or *brutalidad*. In the final itself, the Uruguayans worked a compact formation, whereas the Argentines' nerves seemed strained. Monti, whose rugged play had attracted press criticism and even anonymous death threats, was lackadaisical. Many of the other players also seemed to fear for their safety.

The game seesawed back and forth: 1–0 for Uruguay, 2–1 for Argentina, then 2–2. The home team then began to play with almost wild abandon, netting two more goals. The Argentine federation, disgusted by the result and the events surrounding the final—including violence among the fans—broke off its relationship with the Uruguayans. Internal controversies burst out, too. Monti was accused of being *conejo* (literally, rabbit-hearted). Peucelle admitted, "We never discussed tactics; everybody walked onto the field just thinking he knew what he was supposed to do."

Shots (clockwise) from Uruguay's Pablo Dorado (first half), Pedro Cea, Santos Urdinarán, and Hector Castro (second half) eluded him in Argentina's 4–2 loss.

Fan Fracas

Overexcitement among rival groups of fans has a long history in soccer. Fearing riots between Argentine and Uruguayan fans with more than 20,000 people from Buenos Aires attending the final match in 1930, police carefully searched each spectator, finding knives, pistols, and firearms. Game officials were allowed in the stadium only after all their bags, including the women's purses, had been inspected. John Langenus, the referee, would not accept his role before organizers granted him life insurance and one hundred policemen for his personal safety, an agreement forged only two hours before the scheduled kickoff. Fights did break out among the fans, and Argentina officially protested the incident, withdrawing from all relations with the Uruguayan federation.

1934
Italy

Following the Olympic model, FIFA opted to hold the tournament every four years. In its second edition, the World Cup truly became a worldwide event: thirty-two of the fifty FIFA-affiliated nations were willing to compete. Italy engineered its nomination to host the cup more for political advancement than for sporting purposes. Mussolini's Fascist regime joined the anti-German alliances after Hitler failed in his first attempt to annex Austria to the Reich and believed hosting the tournament had worldwide propaganda value. But the first organizational defeat for the Fascists came when the world champion, Uruguay, refused to participate—repaying the Italians for their absence four years before. The British associations also continued with their boycott. The sixteen teams who did compete in the finals had won earlier qualifying games against the other sixteen teams in the tournament. In Italy the qualifiers continued to compete by direct elimination. The draw for the first round was as follows: Italy vs. the United States, Czechoslovakia vs. Romania, Germany vs. Belgium, Austria vs. France, Spain vs. Brazil, Switzerland vs. Netherlands, Sweden vs. Argentina, and Hungary vs. Egypt. People talked about new styles of soccer, but Vittorio Pozzo, the Italian coach, answered the question, "Everybody is longing for something new, but now on the vigil of the championship, the world becomes old."

There were no surprises on the field. The four favored teams—Germany, Austria, Czechoslovakia, and Italy—were exceptional. Italy best represented the crowd-pleasing qualities of Latin soccer—whimsy and imagination. The Italian team boasted a wide range of athletes, including the South American–born Raimundo Orsi, Enrico Guaita, and the veteran Monti.

The Italian team performs the Fascist salute. Italy vs Czechoslovakia, 1934 World Cup Final (to the right of Combi, the goalkeeper, are Meazza, Orsi, Guaita, and Monti; hidden to his left is Schiavio).

Fascist Windfall

The Italian World Cup was an unprecedented and unexpected financial success. In seventeen matches the total ticket revenues came to $3 million (in 1993 U.S. dollars), for a profit of almost $1 million. The Italian regime sold many tickets by offering travel discounts. Giorgio Vaccaro, a general of the militia, cautiously predicted a deficit so he could then present Il Duce with an organizational and financial success. Every $8 ticket was sold, and the Italian players each received $17,000, which would easily have purchased a house in 1934. The earnings have since risen a great deal: In 1982 players garnered $60,000 for winning the cup; this year, qualifying alone will reap that much.

Reluctant Brilliance

Sometimes even the best soccer talents had to be coaxed into participating. Vittorio Pozzo, a member of Italy's technical staff at the 1912 Olympic games in Stockholm, winner of two straight World Cup titles, and coach of the national team for twenty years, preferred his work as an administrative clerk at Pirelli, the tire company. Because of his reluctance, the Italian federation literally had to force him to accept the coaching position with the Azzurri. A regime man, Pozzo's good psychological attitude, his knowledge of international soccer, and his patriotic devotion and discipline made him the perfect interpreter of soccer under Italian fascism.

FARABOLAFOTO

The semifinals brought the first test of the strongest teams: Italy took on Austria, the famed Wunderteam, which epitomized Danubian-style soccer. The two teams respected each other, as admitted by the Austrian coach, Hugo Meisl: "Italy must certainly be tired after two exhausting matches against Spain," he said. "But I would not be humiliated if Austria should yield." Indeed, Italy had drawn with Spain in the quarterfinals and had made it through by only 1–0 in the replay the very next day.

The Austrians performed a "line-game," using short passes to players moving forward on line with each other and favoring possession. In the quarterfinals they had eliminated their Hungarian neighbors after a violent game. Even Meisl, who was fond of saying, "Soccer is my form of passion," dejectedly observed, "It was not really a football match, but a never-ending quarrel between two teams, neither of which dared to go home." The same intensity characterized the game against Italy. Italy won by a goal scored by the Argentine-born Guaita (which many judged to be offside).

In the second semifinal, Czechoslovakia—another exponent of Danubian soccer—and Germany both played the WM System, discovered by their coaches after a tactics refresher course in England. The victorious Czech team had several Slavia Prague team members, including the goalkeeper Frantisek Planicka, still the most famous Czechoslovakian soccer player (he played in the national team for thirteen years), and Oldrich Nejedly, the enormously gifted top goal scorer of the cup (with five goals, three of them against Germany). Four years later, Nejedly's World Cup career ended when he was hospitalized after enduring the brutal offenses of the Brazilian players who marked him.

In the final, Czechoslovakia reckoned with Italy, whose home crowds, according to French observers, "affected the referee by creating a sense of untenable danger." As the Czech manager, Cesar, dryly commented later, "We would have rather played in Prague." In any case, the Azzurri (so-called because of the color of their shirts) triumphed, due to the brave play of Angelo Schiavio. Not as celebrated in Italian soccer lore as Giuseppe Meazza, Schiavio scored four goals in the cup, including the final's decisive winner in overtime. Elbowing his way into the penalty area, he showed how aggressive play could defeat defenders. He was so effec-

The U.S. player Billy Gonsalvez during his team's 7–1 1934 World Cup first-round loss to Italy.

tive that Vittorio Pozzo moved Meazza to midfield to let Schiavio have more room up front.

A dejected Planicka later admitted, "For a long time, I had thought nobody would ever be able to beat us"; but the political imperative of the Italian mission was reflected in the words of the Azzurri captain, Giampiero Combi, who was "very happy to have kept faith to our promise to the Duce and to the nation."

1938 France

The decision to hold the third World Cup in Europe sparked controversy and led Uruguay and Argentina to boycott the tournament. The political events in Europe also strongly influenced the list of teams willing to play. Spain, deeply engaged in civil war, was not present. But the most serious defection, from the sporting point of view, was Austria: The Wunderteam disappeared along with its country into the expanding German empire. The best players of the Vienna school were later enlisted in the Third Reich's team.

The finals started with thirteen teams plus France (host country) and Italy (defending holder of the world title), the first time the host country and the holder became automatic entrants. England still refused to participate, now on the grounds that its "very superior team" would dominate the competition. This pronouncement was in fact widely accepted by the other nations, who were affected by a sort of inferiority complex about playing British sides until the 1950s. Switzerland, Germany, Poland, Romania, Cuba, Czechoslovakia, Holland, Sweden, Brazil, Norway, and the Dutch East Indies joined the host and defending champions.

Italy was the favorite: Meazza's side held both the Olympic and the world title, but for political reasons the team was strongly disliked by the French supporters. Brazil was a new standout, led by the 25-year-old forward Leonidas da Silva, known for his skills as the Black Diamond. (Brazilian players often are known by their first names or nicknames. Sometimes the nicknames are transferred to other players, who then might have a digit attached to the name they have succeeded to, such as Zito and Zito II.)

The cup immediately brought unexpected results: Germany was eliminated by Switzerland after a replay (1–1; 4–2). Romania was unexpectedly eliminated by Cuba (3–3; 2–1), that country's only time in the finals of the competition.

Leonidas made his great entry on the world stage by scoring a hat trick against Poland, but he found a worthy rival in Ernest Willimowski, who matched him goal for goal. In overtime, after a nearly two-hour battle, Leonidas scored his fourth goal to put Brazil through, 6–5. Italy (2–1 vs. Norway), France (3–1 vs. Belgium), Hungary (6–0 vs. the Dutch East Indies; that country's only time in the finals as well), and Sweden (which advanced without playing, due to the Austrian team's withdrawal) also reached the quarterfinals.

The home team now faced the title holders in Paris in front of sixty thousand spectators. Italy won, 3–1, after goals by Silvio Piola (two) and Gino Colaussi. Brazil and Czechoslovakia also squared off in a brutal game that finished 1–1. Czechoslovakia ended up with only seven men—three were expelled or injured, including the great goalkeeper Planicka with a broken arm and Nejedly with a broken leg—and Brazil, with nine (substitutions were not allowed in international games until 1969–1970).

The South Americans eventually prevailed, due to their strong pool of reserves; they changed nine players for

Left: Giuseppe Meazza, captain of Italy, and Etienne Mattler, captain of France, before Italy's 3–1 victory in the second round of the 1938 World Cup. Below: Italy's Piola (left) puts the first of his two goals past Hungary's Szabo in the 4–2 Italian victory in the 1938 World Cup Final.

reserved the flight from Marseilles).

There the Azzurri faced Hungary, who had beaten Sweden (5–1). On June 19, 1938, at a packed Princes' Park Stadium, the strongly favored Hungarians kicked off. Colaussi scored for Italy after just six minutes, but a minute later Titkos leveled the game. Piola and Colaussi made it 3–1. After 70 minutes, Gyorgyi Sarosi revived his team with a goal, but Piola ended the match (4–2).

Italy had defended the title; even the partisan French crowd seemed willing to forgive political hostilities, and applauded them.

Like the Olympics, the World Cup survived World War II, returning fourteen years later in much the same form. Austria never recovered its prowess—eclipsed now by Hungary—and it was not until 1970 that an Italian team again ascended to the Final.

the replay without diminishing their quality. The Italy vs. Brazil semifinal was played in Marseilles. The South Americans were either so confident that they decided they could afford to play without Leonidas and halfback Tim, who normally supplied vital assists, or else the two players were tired after their hard matches. Leonidas never explained his omission, but Brazil was punished: Italy won 2–1 and flew to Paris (embarrassingly, the Brazilians had been so sure of winning that they had already

1950 World Cup Final: Brazil's Barbosa is beaten by Schiaffino for Uruguay's first goal in the 1–2 upset.

1950

Brazil

The pivotal game of the 1950 World Cup was a confrontation for South American supremacy between Brazil and Uruguay. In the words of the Sky Blue's captain before the final, "There's one chance in a hundred that we shall win; but I don't think it would be right to give up that only chance and start playing with the idea we couldn't do it." The Uruguayan had summed up the premise of the 1950 World Cup, in which Brazil seemed predestined to victory and almost nobody seemed willing to oppose that notion.

Indeed, nobody could imagine an epilogue different from the Green-and-Gold success at the newly built Maracanã Stadium, in front of a rapturous crowd of 200,000. The victory was expected ever since Brazil had been designated as host. Argentina, still disputing with FIFA, had withdrawn its candidacy but offered organizational assistance to its South American neighbor. Thirty-three entrants played the preliminaries to select sixteen teams for Brazil. The four British associations finally abandoned their voluntary exile and participated in the qualifiers for the first time. But only England actually went to the finals—and there the team was a dramatic failure. Sir Stanley Rous, secretary of the English Football Association, acknowledged the postwar realignment of soccer prowess: "I am very discouraged," he said. "If we ever take part in another World Cup, we'll take profit from the lesson we have learned in Brazil."

In the first of the four groups of teams contesting the finals, Brazil overcame Yugoslavia, Switzerland, and Mexico. In the second group, Spain eliminated England, Chile, and the United States, after perhaps the greatest upset in international soccer history. The United States, having fallen far behind in world soccer because it had no professional league, defeated England 1–0.

In group three, Sweden overcame Italy and Paraguay. The fourth group was simply a direct elimination between two teams, Uruguay and Bolivia (8–0). The matches

The Greatest Upset

It seemed at last that the long dispute between FIFA and England had reached a gentleman's agreement when the founders of soccer consented, for the first time, to participate in the 1950 World Cup. They began easily, beating Chile 2–0, but the following match surprised everybody when the U.S. team, including several English and Scottish expatriates, beat them 1–0, on a goal scored by Larry Gaetjens, a player of Haitian origin. When the BBC announced the news, most British listeners assumed there had been an error. (Tragically, Gaetjens is thought to have been executed in 1964 by the special death squads of Haitian dictator Papa Doc Duvalier after being accused of subversive activity.) The U.S. team, like England, did not win another game and did not advance.

Ghiggia and the elegant Juan "Pepé" Schiaffino, for whom July 16, 1950, became a second birthday. In September 1993 he defiantly stated, "I'm only 43. Yes, because I was born on that day." Perhaps the Uruguayans were more tactically aware, whereas Brazil focused more on the players' individual gifts than on the collective aspects of the game.

These two approaches now confronted each other face to face in a world final. Brazil immediately dashed forward, unbridled. Although the Sky Blue resistance was sufficient to produce a balanced first half, Brazil seemed to overcome Uruguay with a goal from Friaça early in the second half. Uruguay eventually recovered its psychological strength, despite the taxing style of the game, and finally reacted: After a series of raids Schiaffino and Ghiggia both scored. Uruguay, to the world's surprise, was the new champion.

were well attended and the games exciting, leading Jules Rimet, the French president of FIFA and one of the principal founders of the World Cup, to comment that the contest had hit its stride: "After the successes obtained by these preparations, I expect to see even more anticipation for the next cup."

The four group winners then faced each other in a newly designed round-robin tournament—as in the qualifiers, the competition granted two points for a win and one for a tie. Thus there was no final per se, but the competition was still as intense, because the last match pitted Uruguay, the more favored of the remaining teams, against the impenetrable Brazil. Brazil demolished Sweden 7–1 and Spain 6–1; Uruguay tied Spain 2–2 and then squeaked past Sweden 3–2. (Sweden beat Spain to secure third place.)

To win the World Cup, Brazil only needed a draw. But Brazil's reputation for attacking soccer was born in this tourna-

ment. The team was paced by Ademir, top scorer in the cup with nine goals. He was explosively fast, and goalkeepers were seemingly flattened by his raking shots. Ademir reinvented the role of forward, striking across the width of the offensive front and daring defenders to chase him down. Supported by a first-rate forward line—Friaça, Zizinho, Jair, and Chico—Ademir and his Brazilian teammates were splendidly overconfident.

The victory feast was ready. After a mass celebrated on the occasion of the win over Sweden, the Brazilian coach, Flavio Costa, announced that on winning the World Cup he would retire to the country. A parade was prepared on Rio's streets, matched only by the celebrated carnival scenes. One of the managers of the Uruguayan team noted abjectly, "For us it would be enough to lose by no more than two goals."

Uruguay's team had its merits, too, displayed best by the intense Alcide "Chico"

Rumors and Riots

Amid the raucous celebration following Uruguay's final win in 1950 to claim the World Cup, an announcement spread in the media from journalist to journalist: Several of the losing Brazilian players had committed suicide. As the news was revealed to be a cruel joke, a real drama exploded in Rio de Janeiro and São Paulo, where the round-robin final round with its South American finale had steadily increased tension levels to a fever pitch. The noise of ambulances carrying injured and dead people rang through the streets, punctuated by gunshots and shouting. Some fans suffered heart attacks, others were literally suicidal, and still others ran riot. Flavio Costa, the Brazilian coach, had to be hidden in order to avoid the fans' vengeance.

1954
Switzerland

One phenomenon, perhaps more than any other, created a new era for soccer in the 1950s: live television broadcasting of matches. As a consequence, the audience expanded exponentially. On July 4, 1954, when the final game of the World Cup tournament was played, the event could be watched live throughout Europe. From that moment, soccer became one of the most followed entertainments in the world.

In an attempt to erase the deep wounds left by World War II, FIFA returned the tournament to Europe. Sixteen finalists met in Switzerland—out of thirty-five federations that took part in the qualifications. Relatively unscathed by the global conflict, Switzerland was the one European country that could guarantee—and afford—the necessary organization. The unqualified favorite was Hungary.

The Magyar had been unbeaten for the previous four years (their last loss had been to Austria, on May 14, 1950). They had won the Olympic laurel in Helsinki in 1952 but, most of all, they had won at Wembley Stadium, the temple of English

soccer, the year before, dispatching the English football "masters" with their first ever defeat at home after almost ninety years of soccer. Six months after that resounding 6–3 victory came another clamorous 7–1 result over England in Budapest.

"Football dressed in new colors," wrote one English commentator, and the world press unanimously described Hungary, with Ferenc Puskas, Sandor Kocsis, Zoltan Czibor, and Nandor Hidegkuti, as the finest team ever to appear on the playing field.

The other finalists represented a global turnout: Yugoslavia, France, Brazil, and Mexico in one group; Hungary, Germany, Turkey, and Korea in the second group; Uruguay, Scotland, Austria, and Czechoslovakia in the third group; England, Italy, Switzerland, and Belgium in the fourth group.

The Hungarians' opening game of the competition reaffirmed their reputation.

South Korea was overmatched 9–0: Kocsis scored three goals. He was even better during the next match, scoring four against West Germany, who went down hard, 8–3. But Hungary's schedule became more difficult. In the quarterfinals and semifinals, Hungary had to play Brazil and Uruguay, respectively.

After being defeated in 1950, the South Americans had introduced a new lineup—

The quarterfinal between Hungary and Brazil (4–2) was one of several pioneering matches televised live from the 1954 World Cup finals.

quite conservative in some ways—based on Djalma and Nilton Santos as outside defenders and on Walter Pereira, Didì and Giulio "Julinho" Botelho—both at the beginning of their formidable careers—as midfielders and forwards. Even though Ferenc Puskas was missing (he was injured badly during the match against Germany), the Hungarians prevailed (4–2). A brawl occurred during the testy game, and the police had to intervene to calm the players down. Astonishingly, Puskas himself, following the game from the sidelines, broke a bottle over Pinheiro's head.

In other progress, England won its group and moved into the quarterfinal, followed by Switzerland. Unbeaten Uruguay and Austria easily controlled Scotland and Czechoslovakia.

Germany moved forward too, but only after a play-off with Turkey to determine the second place in Hungary's group. And Yugoslavia joined Brazil in moving on from that group.

Besides Uruguay, which won 4–2 against the English, Austria reached the semifinals, after a prolific, 7–5 tussle with Switzerland. Germany was a semifinalist as well, after overcoming Yugoslavia 2–0. People expected a Danubian finale.

The Hungarians did eventually dispose of the Uruguayans, with some difficulties (4–2, in overtime), but Germany humiliated its neighbors, due in part to the Austrian goalkeeper's mistakes.

Many unsolved mysteries still surround the final match on July 4. There were rumors about shipments of tractors being sent to Hungary in exchange for throwing the match. There were further rumors about unscrupulous doping by Germans, as jaundice actually struck several of the players who took part in the match.

Beyond these obscure implications, the match played in Bern was no less surprising than that played by Brazil and Uruguay

in 1950. The final ended at 3–2 for the Germans, despite Hungary leading by two goals from Puskas and Czibor after only eight minutes. The Germans struggled back, with quick goals from Max Morlock and Helmut Rahn (after 10 minutes and 18 minutes), but their recovery became a real legend when Rahn again scored 6 minutes from time. A disputable offside call invalidated a goal by Puskas in the final minute.

For the Hungarians, this futile game was their last gesture at the top level of world soccer. They watched as Jules Rimet handed the statuette to the German captain, Fritz Walter, and a new era began.

1958
Sweden

The moment Brazil had awaited for the past eight years came in Sweden in 1958. It was a World Cup in which the South American soccer players' class burst out, making them the unchallengeable, absolute winners. Pelé's star was beginning to glitter: He had made the World Cup team though he was only seventeen; he could already enchant his audience and still cry boyishly with emotion after scoring a goal. The Black Pearl, as he was known, had played for the national team for the first time the year before. Even if his game left people speechless, he was too young to play as a starter. Brazil had an unforgettable, legendary team, where every man was mem-

orable, from Didì to Vavà, from Garrincha to Zito—probably a team without equal. Their coach, Vicente Feola, said, "I could have lined up two different formations, they both would have done." It was a real show for the Swedish audience, whose brief summer was spent immersed in soccer. Italy and Uruguay had surprisingly been stopped in the qualifying rounds, taking away two of Brazil's obstacles. The tournament was composed of West Germany, Czechoslovakia, Ireland, and Argentina (group 1); France, Yugoslavia, Scotland, and Paraguay (group 2); Sweden, Mexico, Hungary, and Wales (group 3); and England, USSR, Brazil, and Austria (group 4).

Brazil paraded a front line of Joel, José Altafini, Didì, and Mario Jorge Lobo "Zagalo" against Austria (3–0). But after tying England, Didì, Nilton Santos, and Juan Bellini strongly insisted on excluding Dino Sani, Altafini, and Joel. There was now room for Pelé, Zito, and Garrincha and a 4-2-4 scheme with the following lineup: Gilmar; de Sordi, Bellini, Orlando, N. Santos; Zito, Didì; Garrincha, Vavà, Pelé, Zagalo. This team also remembered the disillusionment of 1950. Feola reported, "That Brazil was as strong as today's, but I prefer the peaceful Swedish fans to the passionate crowd of Brazil. In 1950 I was part of the technical staff and I suggested a secret withdrawal two days before the final match. They did not want to listen to me."

In group one, West Germany moved

1958 World Cup finals: A goalmouth scramble in the Welsh penalty area during the first-round 1–1 game with Mexico. Goalkeeper Jack Kelsey is on the ground.

1958 World Cup finals: Brazil's Vavà (not seen) scores against Soviet goalie Lev Yashin as Pelé and Zagalo watch the first of Brazil's two goals in the first-round game.

forward. In group two, France and Yugoslavia advanced. The host, Sweden, dominated its group, as did Brazil. The remaining teams to advance were tied on points and so had to compete in play-offs for the final position in their group. England lost to Russia; Wales beat Hungary; Ireland toppled Czechoslovakia. France, West Germany, and Sweden then advanced to the semifinals by beating Ireland, Yugoslavia, and Russia, respectively.

Wales opposed Brazil in the quarterfinals without its best player, John Charles. Pelé scored the only goal of the game. When he saw his team's joy, he burst into tears. Nobody who saw Didì soothing him will ever forget the moment.

There remained only France and Sweden between Brazil and its final tri-

umph. The two teams were surprisingly effective, but there was no comparison with the Green-and-Gold national team: both the semifinal and the final ended 5–2. France needed more than Raymond Kopa, the tournament's best forward, who later joined Real Madrid. (Real's general manager, Saporta, was at the game. Ordered to sign a contract with the best player of the World Cup, he overlooked

the Brazilians and said, "We already have him with us. It is Raymond Kopa.") Not even the other French forward, Just Fontaine, a 13-goal scorer—a record never equaled in a World Cup—could change Brazil's destiny.

Sweden also displayed an enviably talented national team, led by the captain, Nils Liedholm. But Sweden struggled against West Germany in the second

High-Scoring Fontaine

He was called "the Chinese" for his almond-shaped eyes, but Just Fontaine was French and played soccer for Nice and for the national team. In the 1958 World Cup he scored 3 goals against Paraguay, 2 against Yugoslavia, the winning goal against Scotland, and 2 against Northern Ireland. He scored only once in the semifinal against the reigning champions, Brazil, and France lost 5–2. He triumphed again, however, in the third-place final against West Germany, scoring 4 of France's 6 goals, bringing his cup total to 13, still a record for the erstwhile pop singer. Three years later, Fontaine left soccer after a serious leg injury. Next on the top-scorer lists for a single World Cup tournament are Kocsis with 11 goals (1954) and Germany's Müller with 10 goals (1970).

semifinal. Liedholm revealed afterwards, "From the beginning I had told my teammates that we should not play short kicks on line. And I was right. We did not see a ball for the first 30 minutes against the Germans."

In the final Pelé scored two goals, and Vavà scored two. Sweden had put Brazil in arrears for the only time in the tournament when Liedholm scored after three minutes. But from then on the Swedes had to endure an unstoppable Brazil.

To the notes of "goooooooool" sung by South American radio commentators every time Brazil scored, the streets of Rio and of the other South American cities became *torcida:* Reporters said that even while the match was still being played, the fans left their radios to celebrate the joy they had been longing for since 1950. All the tension was now realeased and a new soccer era confidently began. During the award ceremony, Pelé joked with Gilmar: "Hey, my old chap. Why'd you never believe me? I told you we would win."

1962 Chile

In 1962, when the World Cup was held in Chile, Pelé was not an unknown boy anymore. He was to play the starring role in the show, supported by his team. But in the end, the show only partly benefited from his talent. A groin sprain in the second game forced the Black Pearl to be more a spectator than an active participant in the cup. The Brazilians managed worthily by replacing Pelé with Amarildo, and once again the South Americans returned home with the Jules Rimet statuette.

The technical level of the tournament was not particularly high, despite the presence of such players as Puskas (Hungary); Alfredo Di Stefano, Francisco Lopez Gento, and Luis Suarez (Spain); Omar Enrique Sivori, Altafini, and Gianni Rivera (Italy); Lev Yashin and Voronin (USSR);

Bobby Moore, Jimmy Greaves, and Bobby Charlton (England). Indeed, the confluence of players well represented the great but aging masters of Danubian soccer, the Brazilians at the height of their powers, the newly emerging young English core, and distinguished Russian players: a fertile mix of 1950s and 1960s soccer styles.

Brazil played nine of the players from four years before and ended the competition unbeaten with five victories and one draw (0–0 with Czechoslovakia), scoring more goals than any of the other teams and also having the best goal difference (14 for and 5 against). The modest level of competition can be seen in the overall goal average (2.78), which is lower than in all the previous editions and not close to the Swedish average (3.6) or to the record reached in Switzerland eight years before (5.3). Sixteen teams had arrived in Chile. Russia and Yugoslavia had dominat-

Zito celebrates Brazil's second goal past Wilhelm Schroif in the 3–1 victory over Czechoslovakia in the 1962 World Cup.

Brazil's Garrincha (barely visible) cart-wheels between players in the Brazil vs. Chile (4–2) 1962 World Cup semifinal.

Chile. Fans threw back the flowers the Italian players had tossed to them at the start, and the game ended in a brawl in which two Italian players were expelled after reacting to their rivals' aggression.

In the third group, an imperious Brazil swept aside Spain and Mexico, leaving Czechoslovakia and Mexico to battle for the last spot. Despite the Mexicans' win over the Czechs (2–0), it was not enough to compensate for losses to Spain and Brazil. In the last group, Hungary defeated England and Bulgaria and tied Argentina. England picked up the last place for the next round by virtue of a better goal difference than Argentina (whom the English beat 3–1).

In the quarterfinals, Yugoslavia eliminated West Germany by 1–0. Brazil, led by Garrincha and Vavà, marched past England, and Chile finished off Russia 2–1.

Chile's run was stopped by Brazil after another battle. Garrincha, the leader of the Green-and-Gold after Pelé's accident, was injured when a rock thrown by a fan hit him after he had been expelled for retaliating against the fouls of a Chilean defender. Nevertheless, Brazil reached its second consecutive final after overcoming Chile (4–2).

The other side of the draw had revealed, quite unexpectedly, the progress of Czechoslovakia. The maker of this enterprise was a goalkeeper, Wilhelm Schroiff, whose fame is perhaps not as great as it should be. He was the goalie for Slovan Bratislava. The Czechs had performed poorly during the first round (winning just three points and losing to Mexico). In the quarterfinals a goal by Scherer, at 13 minutes, was just enough to weed out Hungary. Schroiff's saves allowed his team to plow on. Even during the semifinal, against Yugoslavia, Czechoslovakia played slowly and deliberately, showing little imagination. Only in the final ten minutes, after extraordinary saves by Schroiff, did the Czechs finally beat the Yugoslavs (3–1).

Before the final, Pelé desperately tried to get himself fit to play, but the medical staff vetoed him. No matter. Josef Masopust equalized after an early Czech goal. Amarildo then became the star of the match, forcing the Czech defense and perfectly placing the go-ahead ball on Zito's head. The final shone with his shots. Vavà effectively ended the match (3–1), and 60,000 Brazilians celebrated.

ed their group, dismissing Uruguay and Colombia with relative ease—though Colombia had fought back from 3–1 down against Russia to tie that game 4–4. Germany and Chile left behind Italy and Switzerland, but not without a fracas. Favoritism toward the home players was more evident here than on previous occasions, and Chile reached the second round after eliminating Italy (2–0), but it was a controversial match: The crowd was particularly hostile to the Italians, since some of the Italian reporters had written about widespread poverty in

Absent Di Stefano

The career of the brilliant forward Alfredo Di Stefano is curious: Despite five European Cups, two Golden Ball awards (most valuable European player for a season), and eleven national championships, he is absent from the annals of the World Cup. Born in Argentina, he spent most of his career in Spain. He never graced the world finals due to a series of unfortunate mishaps: In 1950 Argentina withdrew from the competition; in 1954 the brevity of his newfound Spanish citizenship prohibited him from playing; in 1958 Spain did not qualify; in 1962 he fell ill before the finals. The other brilliant player of Di Stefano's era who also had a limited history in the World Cup is England's Sir Stanley Matthews, who won the first Golden Ball in 1956, at age 41.

1966
England

This was England's moment. England, first through boycott and then through poor results, had not fulfilled its potential. Now the host country had the spotlight and could no longer put off its worldly destiny. The 1966 contest ended in hallowed Wembley Stadium and was settled by the most controversial and mysterious of goals. England was the champion. The coach, Sir Alf Ramsey, had emphatically promised this victory four years before, when he had been given the job to train the team: "England will be the next team to win the World Cup," he announced unequivocally. And right to the night before the final kickoff, the England captain, Bobby Moore, echoed his confidence, "We are sure we are going to win."

Ten European teams competed: France, Portugal, Italy, Spain, West Germany, Switzerland, Hungary, England, Bulgaria, and the USSR. From South America, four teams arrived: Argentina, Uruguay, Brazil, and Chile. Mexico and North Korea flew to England, too. The South Americans were a major disappointment—every team was out by the end of the quarterfinals. The wonderful Brazilians, defending champions from 1958 and 1962, were eliminated in the first round, despite the belief that this was one of the strongest teams. Pelé, Djalma Santos, Garrincha, and other younger players, such as Gerson, Tostao, and Jairzinho, were all there. But when Bulgaria faced Brazil, the Bulgarian defenders savagely worked over the 25-year-old Pelé, and Brazil, without Pelé, went on to lose its next match with Hungary. João Havelange, president of the Brazilian soccer federation at that time, furiously denounced the situation: "We are not going to let Pelé play in the national team again; he would be ruined forever." The great Di Stefano, an expert observer, remarked, "This is too violent a soccer."

A new challenge came from Portugal. This time Pelé played bandaged, and this time the defender Metsi Morais brought him to his knees. Portugal won with a second "black pearl"—Eusebio—shining. The cup's top goal scorer, with nine goals, he was the great protagonist of the tournament. Portugal, in the finals for the first time, reached third place. Eusebio was an extroverted player, tremendously incisive and instinctive: "What do I think of Portugal 4-2-2?" the forward asked rhetorically, "I can't understand: I am not here to think. I am here to play. It is up to the tactics experts to think of numbers." His coach, Otto Gloria, was proud of his players and their methods: "This cup is a physical endurance test. Eusebio did it marvelously. Pelé didn't."

In the quarterfinals, Eusebio's team faced a tough North Korean contingent, which had shocked Italy 1–0 in its group match. (In Italy today a bad loss is still called a "Korean.") Portugal, losing 0–3, beat the

The most controversial goal in history: England's Geoff Hurst (center) and Bobby Charlton (9) appeal for a goal; the West German defenders (including Franz Beckenbauer, 4) call for a corner.

OLYMPIA

Koreans 5–3, but lost to England (2–1) in the semifinal, before beating Russia (2–1) for third place.

After promising to win, England displayed a very "physical" team, but with quick and fanciful players at the same time. Bobby Moore, a wonderful midfielder, and Bobby Charlton, a soccer genius reminiscent of Di Stefano, were the leaders of this team. England had little trouble in its group, before meeting Argentina in the quarterfinals (1–0).

However, objective observers supported West Germany more than England in part because West Germany had discovered its own very young genius, Franz Beckenbauer, a midfielder. Eight years later, in Munich, the "Kaiser" would hold the cup in his hands—but probably never as deservingly as he might have in 1966. West Germany also had such stars as Uwe Seeler,

In the last seconds of overtime, Hurst scores his third goal and England's fourth against West Germany in the 1966 World Cup Final, crowning the host country's victory.

The African Pelé

The first African soccer player of international caliber, Eusebio Ferreira Da Silva, hailed from Mozambique, where he began his career playing for the Lourenço Marques team. During a match in Mozambique, the coach of the Brazilian Ferroviario club, Carlos Bauer, noticed that the young player could run 100 meters in 11 seconds (at that time, the world record was 10 seconds) and was magical with the ball. Bauer spoke with Béla Guttman, the trainer of the Benfica Lisbon team, and Guttman invited Eusebio for a tryout. The legend of the European-African Pelé was born from that first appearance, and Eusebio went on to become the star of Portugal, winning the European Cup with Benfica in 1962, as well as ten national championships and five league cups.

Karl-Heinz Schnellinger, and Wolfgang Overath. But young Beckenbauer, who had begun his career less than one year before, was a special player. There were 20,000 German fans at Wembley on July 31— 100,000 people in all. Germany took the lead first; England equalized and then pulled ahead 2–1. At 90 minutes, Wolfgang Weber reestablished equilibrium. Overtime. Geoff Hurst blasted a shot against the underside of the bar and the ball bounced along the goal line. A German defender kicked it away

for a corner. But the English, as one, exulted at the "goal." The Swiss referee Dienst had not really had a view and ran over to the linesman, who indicated a goal. Hurst then scored again. Queen Elizabeth II presented the World Cup.

The German coach protested, "From the TV shots, everybody will see that it was an irregular goal." And some years later the German weekly *Kicker* reconstructed that sequence with photographs to show that it was not a goal.

OLYMPIA

1970 World Cup Final: Italy's Tarcisio Burgnich cannot stop Pelé heading the first of Brazil's goals in their 4–1 victory.

players' effort were at an advantage. They knew they needed to consider the rarefied atmosphere's effect on the ball speed and the limited endurance of the athletes, and could alter training and game techniques accordingly.

Seventy nations took part in the competition; sixteen made it to the final phase, which was scheduled from May 31 to June 21, 1970. The first round then saw the departures of Israel, Romania, Belgium, El Salvador, Sweden, Czechoslovakia, Bulgaria, and Morocco from the tournament.

The Mexican team was treated perhaps with a "respectful eye" and reached the quarterfinals after defeating Belgium by virtue of a very dubious penalty kick. There, however, they were eliminated by Italy (4–1). In the first round Brazil beat England (1–0) in a game that saw Pelé and Rivelino match their abilities against those of Bobby Moore and goalkeeper Gordon Banks. Banks's spectacular save from a seemingly unstoppable Pelé header is still considered one of the most memorable duels in soccer.

An improving Peru, coached by the Brazilian Didì, faced its coach's countrymen, but Brazil won easily (4–2). The quarterfinals also staged a replay of London's final, England vs. West Germany. After the endless controversies over Hurst's goal, the Germans had the opportunity of a return match. But this time there seemed to be no balance: The defending champions quickly scored two goals. After Bobby Charlton and Martin Peters were substituted for defenders, Franz Beckenbauer and Uwe Seeler gradually worked Germany back into the game. At 90 minutes the score was 2–2. In overtime, the decisive shot came from a center forward who did not look very athletic, but who possessed a goal-scorer's instinct. He even wore number 13, which players traditionally refused for superstitious reasons. With 10 goals, Gerd Müller became the top scorer of this tournament.

If England vs. West Germany brought out strong sentiments, the semifinal between Italy and Germany will be long

1970 World Cup Final: Pelé and Brazil (Gerson and Carlos Alberto are either side of Pelé) retire the Jules Rimet Trophy after Brazil's third championship.

1970
Mexico

Two wonderful adventures ended in Mexico in 1970: The Jules Rimet Trophy found its permanent home in Brazil and Pelé departed the international stage after conquering his third world prize, twelve years after his debut in Sweden.

For Pelé, it was the last step in the making of the legend. He became the only player to have won three world titles. "O'Rey," the soccer king bearing number ten on his shirt, was in the descending phase of his career by the Mexico cup, and some Brazilian critics would have liked to have seen him omitted from the *Seleçao*

(national team). But the coach, Zagalo (one of the main players in Brazil's victories in the past), preferred to utilize an attack without pure forwards, except Tostao. The scheme was full of fanciful midfielders, all of whom wore the number 10 shirt for their clubs. Jairzinho, Roberto Rivelino, Pelé, and Gerson not only succeeded in playing together but were lethal for rival defenses.

This Brazilian team scored more than any other: 19 goals in 6 games, with an average of 3.16 goals per match. It was also the team that could boast the best goal difference (plus 12), allowing only 7 goals to be scored against them.

Many of the matches in Mexico were played at high altitude. The final was played in Mexico City, 7,218 feet above sea level. Those federations that studied the effects of the environment on the remembered as one of the most intense matches in soccer history. Oddly, most of the two scheduled halves were not extremely exciting: A goal from Roberto Boninsegna put Italy ahead from the very beginning, but in the last minute the Germans drew level. Schnellinger scored —ironically, he was playing in Italy for A.C. Milan at the time.

The overtime sequel then began. Müller scored the go-ahead goal at 94 minutes; Tarcisio Burgnich equalized after 98 minutes; Luigi Riva scored to make it 3–2 at 103 minutes; Müller, again, equalized at

Scandal in Bogotá

"Bogotá" remains something of a dirty word in English soccer circles after an unfortunate incident immediately preceding the 1970 World Cup Final in Mexico. Champions in 1966 and very highly rated in 1970, the English team flew to Colombia to play a friendly match but were waylaid after a jeweler announced the theft of a gold bracelet following a visit by English players.

Upon inquiry, the Colombian police charged Bobby Moore, the captain of the English team, with the crime, arresting him on the spot. Only after posting bail was Moore released. Upon his arrival in Mexico, Pelé visited Moore to voice his support. The English, however, still cast a suspicious eye on Colombia.

OLYMPIA

109 minutes. Was it over? No indeed. After kicking off, Rivera charged forward, Boninsegna's piercing long pass reached him, and he flashed a shot past Sepp Maier: 4–3 at 110 minutes. Brazil's demonstrative semifinal triumph (3–1) over Uruguay (which had beaten Russia 1–0 in the quarterfinals) was almost soporific by comparison.

But Brazil was to have the cup. They were unquestionably superior to the Italians. Pelé seemed to reach the sky when he headed the first goal after 18 minutes. Boninsegna gave Italy an illusory 1–1, but goals from Gerson, Jairzinho, and Carlos Alberto ended the match. Pelé, wearing a sombrero, brought home his third cup, a trophy that has been retired to Brazil for having been the first team to win it three times.

1974
Germany

Munich 1974 stood for "total soccer," soccer in which every player could play every position. In the FIFA gold book register, this was West Germany's competition—winner and host country. Endowed with such first-rate veteran players as Müller, Beckenbauer, and Maier, West Germany was a splendid team. But the whole world was enchanted by Johan Cruyff's Holland, the archetype of total soccer. The Dutch team also revolutionized what life could be outside the game. The players were always accompanied by their wives rather than isolating themselves in hotels. Cruyff was confident: "We are the best. And please, let's not speak about the South Americans' game. Their game is so slow, it's absurd. I'd rather play Zaire and Haiti, though I don't think *I* will ever equal Pelé."

Of the World Cups, Munich 1974 most keenly felt the new political influence of the Third World. The Brazilian João Havelange was elected president of FIFA. With support from the African countries, he overcame the other candidate, England's Sir Stanley Rous. There were sixteen finalists divided into four groups, with newcomers Zaire and Haiti present: East Germany, West Germany, Chile, and Australia (Group A); Brazil, Yugoslavia,

Italy's Sandrino Mazzola scores against Argentina in the 1–1 first-round game in the 1974 World Cup finals.

West German chancellor Willy Brandt and U.S. Secretary of State Henry Kissinger at the 1974 World Cup Final.

Scotland, and Zaire (B); Holland, Sweden, Uruguay, and Bulgaria (C); Poland, Argentina, Italy, and Haiti (D).

West Germany put together an enviable team. The European champions could boast an extraordinary defense: Maier, the schooled goalkeeper; Paul Breitner, an intimidating defender (who was called "the Maoist" because of his political sympathies) whose tackles were deadly; Beckenbauer, the elegant *libero*, in his fourth World Cup finals, who directed attacks from deep inside his own half, revolution-

izing the traditional defensive role; and the implacable forward, Gerd Müller, in his third tournament. With four goals, Müller sped Germany into the final match, closely assisted by Breitner with three goals. However, West Germany's two victories before the final were tarnished by an upset loss to their "poor cousins," the East Germans. Paradoxically, it was a useful defeat because it allowed the Germans to have an easier draw in the semifinals. Yet Beckenbauer publicly acknowledged the team's problems: "Our training is too

hard. The training camp is a sort of concentration camp. I am saying this for all my comrades. We are not serene. The Dutch are even allowed to leave their camp."

Holland's play was epitomized by Cruyff, who was probably the greatest European player of the 1970s, an extraordinary forward with intoxicating dribbling skills and a great instinct for goals. Cruyff's personality was difficult at times. He often imposed his choices on his team, backed up by his coach, Rinus Michels, one of the Ajax Amsterdam coaches, whom Cruyff had followed to F.C. Barcelona in 1973. Michels solved one of the team's problems by sending Piet Keizer to the bench, exactly as Cruyff had asked. "We are a family, and we have quarrels like every family has. But there is also a sense of comradeship," claimed Michels. Thus, despite their progress, both Holland and West Germany suffered from dissension.

The road to the final was easy for Holland. Just one goal conceded, five overwhelming victories, and only one

Holland's Cruyff is tripped for a penalty by Uli Hoeness after a long run into the area in the first minute of the 1974 World Cup Final.

OLYMPIA

Left: Holland's Cruyff and West Germany's Beckenbauer in the 1974 World Cup Final.
Below: Victorious West Germans after their 1974 World Cup championship: (right to left) Flohe, Müller, Breitner, and Schwarzenbeck.

draw—to a surprisingly alert Sweden. Before the final in Munich, observers and bettors favored Holland. The result seemed preordained: after one minute, Cruyff was knocked down in the penalty area. His brother-in-law, Jan Neeskens, scored from the spot kick. Was everything to be so easy? Germany reacted proudly and furiously. Breitner scored on a penalty kick and the implacable Müller's sixty-eighth goal for Germany gave the victory to the Whites. In an allusion to the 1954 World Cup Final, Helmut Schoen, the 1974 German coach, later said, "I wanted my players to read the statements made by the Dutch before the match: that was our only doping." The revelation of the tournament was Poland (with Kazimierz Deyna, Robert Gadocha, Gregorz Lato, Tomaszewski, and Gorgon), which had beaten a declining Pelé-less Brazil. The Polish coach, Gorki, was enthusiastic: "My team is putting into practice what I have been studying at my desk."

1978
Argentina

OLYMPIA

The star of the eleventh issue of the World Cup had long black hair and wore the colors of the host country. His name was Mario Kempes, and Argentina idolized him for the first twenty-five days of June 1978. Marito, as he was called by the Argentine fans, was the first player to be a world champion and top scorer in the tournament. Before the competition, the organizers had feared the politicization of the cup. Two years before the kickoff, a putsch, led by General Jorge Videla, had consigned power to the Argentine army. Fortunately, the country's outpouring of enthusiasm for soccer avoided the transformation of the FIFA World Cup into Videla's World Cup.

The international federation had set up a daunting qualification system. There were 106 national teams in the qualifiers: 90 of them were eliminated, leaving the

remaining 16 to meet in South America at the end of the Argentine fall. Many of the greatest teams were not as strong as expected: Germany had lost its most charismatic players, including Beckenbauer, Müller, Hoeness, and Breitner. Holland was there, but without Cruyff, and Italy and Brazil, following their 1974 disappointments, did not seem, at least on paper, to have rebuilt their teams. England, like four years earlier, did not even qualify.

Surprisingly, Italy had a perfect first-round record, including the defeat of Argentina, 1–0. France and Hungary failed to advance, after both were beaten by Argentina. Poland and West Germany mixed it up with Tunisia and Mexico.

Despite strong showings by the Tunisians, they bowed on points eventually to the Europeans, despite drawing with West Germany. Austria and Brazil overcame Sweden and Spain in the third group,

Above: 1978 World Cup Final: In over-time, Luque (left) celebrates Kempes's (center) second goal against Holland in Argentina's 3–1 victory.
Right: Argentina's famed Rio Plata stadium at the end of the 1978 World Cup Final.

and Peru and Holland bypassed Iran and Scotland in the final group. Holland, runners-up in 1974, but now without Cruyff—who resisted his team's invitation to play—did not look at all impregnable, having lost 3–2 to Scotland and playing Peru to a 0–0 draw.

Indeed, future talents were already

growing. Michel Platini led a young team from France. In the first round, these *bantams* had yielded to Argentina (but with many doubtful calls by the referees), and then to Italy.

Italy had a very young forward in Paolo Rossi. Coach Enzo Bearzot's Italian team had beaten the Argentines in Buenos

Aires, forcing them to go to Rosario for the second round—another round-robin procedure—together with Brazil and Poland, while Peru, Italy, Austria, Germany, and Holland remained in Buenos Aires, the capital of Argentina, but now without the host.

The first team in each of the two groups would go to the final; the second team would play for third and fourth place. It was a criticized formula because it created a suspicious atmosphere—indeed, it was abandoned four years later. Because teams played for points and goal averages, the timing of the matches played an inordinately significant role. For instance, Argentina started playing against Peru after the result of Brazil vs. Poland was known. Kempes and his comrades knew they needed six goals to overcome Brazil on goal difference—and that was the final result. While Argentina was in delirium, the Brazilians were indignant with FIFA. At the same time, Italy and Holland were playing their match. The Dutch needed only a draw. The Italians led during the first part of the game but eventually conceded two goals, and Holland reached its second consecutive final.

Holland had revived by the second round, with West Germany and Austria falling far behind. Poland and Peru, dominant in the early round, now also seemed to struggle, letting Brazil and Argentina control the group.

Once the finalists were set, two teams who would again face off in an epic game in 1982 remained to play the penultimate game, in which the Italian team was upset by Brazil for third place (2–1).

One billion television viewers joined eighty thousand live spectators to watch Argentina and Holland in the overflowing Rio Plata stadium. The Europeans played at a fast pace, but they could not find the right opening for a decisive shot; the South Americans were in Kempes's hands. The man with the flowing mane took his team into the lead at 38 minutes. Dirk Nanninga drew Holland level at 81 minutes, but, for the second time, Holland was to lose the cup.

And how it did! At the last minute Rob Rensenbrink devoured half of the Dutch defense in gulps and kicks, the picture of an exuberantly confident winner. The ball hit the goalpost, taking the game into overtime. Again Kempes was still the best, bringing the score to 2–1 at 104 minutes. Then Daniel Bertoni (114 minutes) started the party. The cry *"Argentina campeón"* rang throughout Buenos Aires.

1982 Spain

A name traversed the world in the summer of 1982: Paolo Rossi, who was given the nickname Pablito Mundial. The Azzurri forward scored six goals in the last three matches (three vs. Brazil, two vs. Poland in the semifinal, one vs. Germany in the final); he earned Italy its third title after Italy had barely survived the first round—and qualified only because of its goal difference against Cameroon. Spain 1982 had seemed to have a fated winner: the Brazil of Zico, Paulo Falcao, Toninho Cerezo, Socrates, and Junior. Their coach, Tele Santana, had studied and practiced various European schemes, but preferred to let his players be as fanciful as ever. And not to be discounted were Maradona's Argentina and Platini's France. Yet every forecast was to be turned upside down.

Twenty-four teams now played in the expanded final round, divided into six groups: Italy, Poland, Cameroon, and Peru; West Germany, Austria, Algeria, and Chile; Belgium, Argentina, Hungary, and El Salvador; England, France, Czechoslovakia, and Kuwait; Northern Ireland, Spain, Yugoslavia, and Honduras; and Brazil, the USSR, Kuwait, Scotland, and New Zealand. Italy provided the first surprise. The team was physically unfit and morale was low. Italy's coach, Enzo Bearzot, had regained Paolo Rossi only two months earlier, after the player's yearlong disqualification for taking part in a game-fixing scandal.

During the first round, Rossi was a ghost of his former playing self. Any other coach would have excluded him from the team, but Bearzot was apparently overly grateful to Rossi and to other players for

Italy's progress in the 1982 World Cup met with increasing acclaim at home.

the inspiring 1978 Argentine Mundial. "I have not been able to find a better Rossi," he retorted. Facing an avalanche of press criticism, the players decided to boycott the media. Bearzot supported them: "They are free citizens, they are not my employees." The 40-year-old goalkeeper, Dino Zoff, was more explicit: "We just feel bombed from everywhere. We are not strong enough to do without the press—we know it—but we had to do something about [their behavior]."

Italy eked its way into the second round only by scoring one goal more than Cameroon. The criticism was unabated. After the disheartening draw, Rossi admitted, "I've been running without aim, and it has never been so depressing." To make matters worse, Italy was drawn in the round-robin with Brazil and Argentina. A perceptive Maradona warned, "The Italians frighten me more than anybody else." But nobody, it seemed, would stop Brazil. Brazil's and Roma's Paulo Falcao was

Throwing the Game

One World Cup scandal occurred in the round-robin group of 1982 between West Germany, Austria, Algeria, and Chile. Only two teams could move to the next round. The Germans were defeated by the Algerians, headed by their top scorer, Rabah Madjer, nicknamed "Allah's Heel," and by playmaker Lakhder Belloumi. But under the 2-1-0 points formula, for the group's last match Austria had a better goal difference than Algeria and so could afford to lose by a goal to their German colleagues; this way, both West Germany and Austria could qualify. The Germans nefariously triumphed 1–0 over a deliberately casual Austria, and both advanced. West Germany reached the final; Austria was knocked out in the second round. Algeria's protest was not sustained.

3–2 over Brazil in a second-round game Italy had to win to advance.

2–0 over Poland in the semifinal, after two goals by Rossi.

3–1 over West Germany in the final, bringing Italy its third championship.

confident: "We are more than just a team. Even if Italy isn't a *squadra materasso* [literally, "mattress team," meaning totally ineffective]."

In the round-robin second round to select semifinalists, Poland escaped on goal difference over Russia (Belgium lost

Italy's Rossi (left) and Antonio Cabrini and Brazil's Falcao (who played at club level with Italy's Roma) in second-round game.

to both); West Germany advanced over England and Spain; France dominated Austria and Northern Ireland—which had become the leading British team for a short era. The remaining group consisted of Italy, Brazil, and Argentina.

Brazil had dominated its qualifying round, easily dispatching the USSR, which, according to some critics, was playing the soccer of the twenty-first century. On the other hand, Argentina, the world champi-

on, had been disappointing. They lost to Belgium, and Maradona succeeded in getting himself expelled. He was only 21 and clearly could not keep up with all the responsibilities weighing on him: "I'm just like every other man," he confessed in mid-tournament. "I can't take on any more responsibilities." Zico vs. Maradona; Brazil vs. Argentina: that was still anticipated as the true "final."

When Italy's turn came, the impossible

commenced. Argentina was defeated after an implacable Azzurri defender, Claudio Gentile, tightly marked Maradona—a performance that made soccer history. Italy vs. Brazil was the last match to decide the semifinalists. The Brazilians needed to draw, but Italy was uncontainable. Rossi scored, Brazil equalized, Rossi again, Brazil again, and Rossi again! Then, as happens in tournaments, Italy suddenly sensed that the rest would be easy: winning first against Poland in the semifinals, 2–0, and defeating a Germany that was worn out by the match against France, which ended in penalty kicks after West Germany had magnificently recovered from being 3–1 down in overtime. Italy was the world champion.

Tardelli celebrates after scoring Italy's second goal in the 3–1 win over West Germany in the 1982 World Cup Final.

France's Platini in midair during the 1986 World Cup

1986
Mexico

In this foot game, a handball causes a sensation: Perhaps not surprisingly, it was Maradona's hand that hit the ball and scored the goal, leaving Peter Shilton, the veteran English goalkeeper—the most capped player ever—completely astonished. Asked to explain the travesty, the Argentine star famously quipped at the post-match press conference, "It was the hand of God." That episode became the most famous symbol of the 1986 cup, played in Mexico (like sixteen years earlier) after Colombia, the intended organizers, withdrew. Mexico did well, especially given that an earthquake had devastated the country eighteen months earlier, exacerbating the country's already difficult economic problems. Once again, the matches were played at high altitude. After the 1970 experience, all the federations were alert and better prepared their teams by employing various scientific methods to cope with the consequences of limited oxygen. Maradona, now in his prime, was expected to become an athlete who could change the destiny of a match. He was quickly forgiven for his handball against England because only moments later he proved that he had other ways to score, as only he could do. He recovered a ball in center field and started to slalom through the English defense. As his run accelerated into a turbocharged finale, he skipped over opponents as if they were ninepins, leaving no fewer than six of them, goalkeeper included, behind—carnage in his wake—as he laid the ball into the empty goal and committed himself to the endless applause of the Azteca stadium.

The statistics of this World Cup, late in the twentieth century, are astronomical: 4.2 billion people watched it worldwide. A satellite named after a Mexican hero, Morelos, broadcast the images of the 528 players to 170 countries all over the globe. Some 1,750 journalists followed the event. And in the squares of the biggest Mexican cities, up to 1,600 gallons of beer were consumed nightly. The world, it might be said, was all part of the show.

Italy was not the magical team of 1982. Paolo Rossi was there but never took the field. Rather, the competition's destiny depended on two champions: Maradona and Platini. They both played for Italian clubs (Napoli and Juventus of Turin, respectively). Among the dark horses, Denmark and the USSR were strong: the former composed mainly of mercenaries from foreign clubs, and the latter famous for its avant-garde tactics in which players ranged the field, free of designated positions.

Soviet coach Valeri Lobanowski's players were eventually turfed out by Belgium in the second round (4–3 in overtime) after endless discussions about two Belgian goals that were suspected to have been offside, while the Danes had an off day in that round, losing 5–1 to Spain after conceding four goals by Emilio Butragueño. Brazil proceeded easily into the quarterfinals, facing France immediately after that country's victory over Italy. The South American's Zico missed a penalty kick and the teams

BOB THOMAS/RICHIARDI

With his hand, Argentina's Maradona scores first of his two goals against England's Peter Shilton in the 1986 World Cup quarterfinal.

were forced into overtime and, finally, penalty kicks. Platini missed his kick, but the Brazilians still lost.

West Germany was not enchanting anybody, but it continued to advance. In the second round against Morocco, Germany was saved in injury time by Lothar Matthäus's goal. In the quarterfinals Mexico and Germany went into penalty kicks. The home team was overburdened by the pressure, and the Germans reached the semifinal, beating France 2–0.

After his enterprising tactics against England, Maradona gave another show, this time for Belgium's benefit in the semifinal. The Pibe de Oro scored twice, taking his team to the ultimate challenge. On June 29, with the vast Azteca stadium sold out, Argentina went two up, with goals by José-Luis Brown and Jorge Valdano. Maradona, tightly marked by Matthäus, disappeared from whole chapters of the game. Still, with 20 minutes left, everything seemed resolved. But the German pride was rising.

In 8 startling minutes, from 73 minutes to 81 minutes, Karl-Heinz Rummenigge and Rudi Voeller scored for Germany, pulling themselves level with their adversaries. Was everything to change? Almost. Two minutes later, Jorge Burruchaga received a brilliant Maradona assist and scored. It was Argentina's eulogy, and Maradona was crowned in the stadium that had seen

Pelé's last triumph.

As a footnote—Maradona now had reserved his place in the history books— the "hand of God" episode continued to haunt him. Playing the USSR in the first round in 1990, he stopped a shot on the Argentine goal line with his hand. He again explained that at such tense moments, his hands were not in his control!

Penalty Shots

Brazil's 1986 team was one of that country's best ever. When France faced them in the quarterfinals, a 1–1 draw after overtime necessitated a penalty shoot-out to decide the match. After the first two of five for each team, French player Bruno Bellone's kick hit the post and then goalkeeper Carlos's back, settling finally into the net. Romanian referee Ion Igna sanctioned the goal, despite the rule that only a direct shot can score in a penalty series. When the protesting Brazilian center back, Julio Cesar, missed his shot after the endless dispute, Brazil was eliminated. After the cup, FIFA clarified that Bellone's shot was legal. France then lost to West Germany in the semifinal, for the second World Cup in a row.

Rummenigge shoots past Neri Pumpido for West Germany's first goal in the 3–2 loss to Argentina in the 1986 World Cup Final.

1990
Italy

After 56 years, the World Cup returned to Italy. Observers might be forgiven for thinking it was just a realigned league championship due to the enormous economic power of the Italian football clubs, who had most of the world's stars already under contract. Germany was led by Lothar Matthäus, Inter Milan's midfielder. He was no longer the obscure halfback who played Maradona in Mexico City's final, but rather the leader of a powerful German

A farewell to Italia '90 from Cameroon's Indomitable Lions after 3–2 quarterfinal loss to England. (Most have traded their shirts for England's, an international tradition after games.)

team coached by former champion Franz Beckenbauer. Holland, the reigning European champion, bet on the strengths of its star trio—Ruud Gullit, Marco Van Basten, and Frank Rijkaard, all hailing from the Italian club A.C. Milan. Maradona, Mexico's hero, renewed his reign in

Naples: he was worshipped by the city that had claimed two club championships on the force of his talents. Brazil itself, another favorite on the eve of the cup, had as its center forward Careca, who had played for Napoli with "Dieguito." As in every World Cup, the host team was one

of the favorites. Italy certainly had the necessary qualities to occupy the pole position for Italia '90.

The trend of the tournament was visible after the very first match: The defending champions were beaten by Cameroon—a startling result, because African soccer was still considered to be unsophisticated. It is not an overstatement to say that Cameroon's François Omam-Biyik's goal opened new horizons for the soccer planet. Cameroon proved that it was not just a flash in the pan. The team reached the quarterfinals and only lost to England in overtime, hampered by a sparse defense that had been depleted by suspensions. Thirty-eight-year-old Roger Milla, called into his country's team at the last minute—over the objections of the coach—was one of the finest and most dangerous players in the tournament.

In eliminating Sweden and Scotland, Costa Rica also showed new possibilities, whereas Argentina and Holland had a hard time advancing. Both reached the direct elimination matches on goal difference. Four potential finalists faced each other in the second round: Germany vs. Holland and Brazil vs. Argentina. By chance, the European match was played in Milan, at San Siro. Holland's Gullit, Van Basten, and Rijkaard played for A.C. Milan at club level, and Germany's Matthäus, Jürgen Klinsmann, and Andreas Brehme played for Inter Milan. Splitting Milanese fans' loyalties, the match between Germany and Holland was like one of those troubling "derbies," games in which two teams from the same city are pitted against one another. Germany prevailed with goals scored by two Inter Milan players.

The South American match took place in Turin, with Brazil as the favorite. Argentina seemed less than impressive: The first phase of the cup had revealed Argentina's limitations, and Maradona was having problems with one of his ankles. The game languished without a goal until 8 minutes before the end, when Maradona distinguished himself—for the only time in the game—with a brilliant zigzag through the Brazilian defense, culminating in what writer Pete Davies called "an impossibly perfect" pass to Claudio Caniggia, who scored. Brazil, disappointed again, returned home without making the quarterfinals.

Playing in Florence, Argentina appeared

Holland's Frank Rijkaard and Germany's Rudi Voeller before being sent off. Germany won the second-round game, 2–1.

OLYMPIA

Soccer's Cinderella

The Cinderella of soccer, Salvatore Schillaci, an Italian forward known as Totò, played in the World Cup only three months after being picked for the first time to play on the Italian national team. He entered the game against Austria with only 15 minutes left, scoring the decisive goal 4 minutes after his World Cup debut. His goal against Ireland put Italy into the semifinal. Totò was the hero of the so-called "magic nights" and after the third match he was a regular starter. In the end, he was the top scorer of the tournament with six goals. Sadly, he was not able to replicate those magic nights in future Italian championships. He withdrew from international soccer one year later; he now plays for Inter Milan.

to spare its energies against Yugoslavia, and a 0–0 score after 120 minutes brought the two teams to penalties. Maradona missed his kick and incurred the noisy wrath of the crowd, but the Yugoslavians did even worse and Argentina won 3–2. A scorer in the Paolo Rossi vein and a recent addition to the Italian team, Totò Schillaci, was decisive in Italy's 1–0 win over Ireland, setting the stage for Italy's semifinal match against Argentina. West Germany and England were to face off in the other semifinal after West Germany easily defeated Czechoslovakia 1–0, and England squeaked by Cameroon, beating them in overtime 3–2 and only after being awarded two penalty kicks on fouls against the elusive Gary Lineker. Despite their loss, the Indomitable Lions of Cameroon left the competition amid an unusual burst of appreciative cheering for their overall performance in the tournament.

Italy and Argentina played in front of a Naples crowd that was unsettled about how to respond to Maradona, the local Napoli team's hero, as he faced Italy. Italy's Schillaci began the scoring. Shortly after, Caniggia evened the game, putting the first goal of the World Cup past goalkeeper Walter Zenga. From this point, Italy was doomed. The game went inevitably to penalty kicks and the extraordinary Argentine goalkeeper, Sergio Goycoechea, blocked two shots, defeating the distraught Italians.

At the same time, West Germany defeated England, also in penalty kicks. On July 8, Italy triumphed over England for third place.

In a repeat of the 1986 final, West Germany braced itself against Argentina, ready to avenge its earlier loss. The Argentines began at a disadvantage, having been forced to give up their star forward, Caniggia, and four other players to disqualification. The Mexican referee Eduardo Codesal Mendez was second-rate. He made several poor and hotly contested calls, sent off two Argentines, and awarded Germany a questionable penalty kick that cost Argentina the game: with Andreas Brehme's conversion, West Germany won 1–0.

Lineker of England, top scorer in Mexico 1986, shows a goal scorer's instincts in clawing past Ireland's Bonner, McCarthy, and Morris in the 1–1 first-round 1990 game. Following pages: Germany's Kohler (center), Matthäus (right), and Buchwald with the 1990 FIFA World Cup after 1–0 victory over Argentina.

England vs. Germany, 1990 World Cup semifinal. "A dog of war with the face of an angel": England's Paul Gascoigne weeps after a yellow card eliminates him from potential role in the final.

1994
USA

The world chose the twenty-four participants for USA 1994—twenty-two, to be precise, because the United States (host) and Germany (defending champion) have known their destiny for some time. The other 170 countries were involved in the most combative qualifications in history. Starting with Europe, surprises were not lacking. At least three results were calamitous: the elimination of all four British teams, the incredible KO of France in the very last minute of their last qualifying game, and the coup de grâce for Denmark, so briefly the champions of Europe. England was pushed out, punished, above all, by their limiting tactical methods and the intolerant atmosphere surrounding coach Graham Taylor. Taylor's resignation was followed by the Professional Footballers Association demanding a government inquiry into the state of the English game. A worse fate, perhaps, fell to France, for which a tie in just one of its last two home games would have been enough to qualify. France seemed to have wrapped up Bulgaria, 1–0. Then the cracks appeared: The Bulgarians tied the score with minutes left, and their forward Emil Kostadinov scored a *eurogol*—a spectacular winner—in the 90th minute. With France in tears, the coach, Gerard Houllier, resigned, and speculation focused on the appointment of former coach and World Cup star Platini. Because the next World Cup will be played in France, it is not possible for them to fail next time. Denmark paid for its inability to score and was overcome by a rejuvenated Spain. Ireland, coached by Jack Charlton, the only Englishman who will go to the United States, will hope to improve on its successful 1990 run.

Two favorites just made it: Italy, troubled in its group by the Swiss (another surprise) and the Portuguese; and Holland, deprived of Van Basten and obliged to surrender first place to an astonishingly strong Norway. The Norwegian team under Drillo Olsen was perhaps the best coached team: no stars but an extraordinary group—to be feared. "Norway," said

one British commentator, "found a team." Sweden, Belgium, Romania—with an explosive attack—Russia and Greece (thanks to the disqualification of Yugoslavia in its rotation) also passed the test. Greece qualified for the first time ever; Norway qualified for the first time since 1938. In three of these European groups, the two qualifiers were selected on the last day of the round. Ireland, Spain, Italy, Switzerland, Belgium, and Romania all fulfilled their ambitions on the same day. The most tense game was perhaps in Cardiff, where Wales missed a penalty kick in its 2–1 loss to Romania.

From the rest of the world the signs of innovation are plentiful. In South America the most convincing team is Colombia's. Their forward Faustino Asprilla could be the 1994 American star. Brazil made it with the steady Romario but with a lot of problems for the contentious coach, Carlos Alberto Parreira. Bolivia took advantage of the home matches played at 10,900 feet in La Paz to assure itself of qualification upsets against Brazil and Uruguay. Argentina—winners in 1978 and 1986 and finalists in 1990—were

Jakobsen passing England's Adams. Norway left behind a strong group in its surprising run to the World Cup finals.

reduced to a 1–0 own-goal victory in the second leg of a play-off against Australia (the teams had tied 1–1 in Sydney). An unfit Maradona, often walking in the games, nevertheless led his team to the finals—his fourth world championship. Mexico also retrieved another restless veteran, Hugo Sanchez, to bring Mexico to the United States.

Africa advanced, with Cameroon and Morocco making their third championships. But Nigeria announced itself as the strongest team, with its contingent of players scattered among European clubs. Despair spread across Asia after Japan gave up a goal in the last minute of the final qualifier to Iraq, and so was out. Japan will have to revise its plans—it wanted to organize the World Cup in 2002, but it now seems a less likely choice. Saudi Arabia and South Korea qualified, but they do not seem formidable opponents. Iran and Iraq—and even North Korea—might have qualified, causing momentary fear among U. S. State Department officials, but their threats evaporated in the Asian qualifying matches. The media focused on these political match-ups, but as with Ireland's final game against Northern Ireland in Belfast, political hostility was transcended by soccer and fair play.

BOB THOMAS/RICHIARDI

The Fans

Pelé called it the beautiful game, and it is a game of love, passion—and fans. The fans make the game. The terraced steps (now being replaced by all-seating stadiums) on which they stand and sing great choruses of support; the fanzines (unofficial publications with the best gossip and news about a team); the seas of scarves and flags—these are the phenomena that define soccer at Wembley, San Siro, Nou Camp, and the Maracanã. But soccer in some countries suffers from obsolete stadiums and from a worse infection: youths who are thugs, attracted by the prospect of violence. They are called "hooligans," and they have endangered the fabric of the game. In Denmark, by contrast, they are boastful of their *roligans,* from the word *rolig,* which in Danish means tranquil. A multicolored mass, faces all painted in white and red, spent midsummer 1992 in song. In June 1992 the Danish national team took a boat to Stockholm. They arrived by chance at the European Championship finals, promoted only as a result of a painful political choice—the exclusion of Yugoslavia. The Danish populace had no more pretenses than the team. But Denmark's successes grew on and off the field. While the most esteemed European teams struggled, Denmark marched into the final. While the English supporters battled with the police and destroyed the host city, the *roligans* were making friends, having drinks with their opponents, and cheering in the most tranquil manner possible. On winning the cup and creating the fairy tale, the Danish athletes threw themselves into the arms of their supporters. Another 100,000 people waited for their heroes in the main square of Copenhagen, and the beer mixed with the tears.

Tears have always soaked sporting events. Sadly, the disappointments can be more than a slight shower of rain. The Brazilian *torcida* are the most admired fans in the world. Every country that hosts the World Cup is invaded by a Green-and-Gold swarm. Real orchestras play the samba continuously on the sidelines; splendid dancers are immortalized by the cameramen. There is never a shadow of sadness. Only the team can throw the *torcida* into distress. They have not won a title since 1970. In the last three tournaments the South Americans were among the favorites. After the games with Italy in Barcelona (2–3) in 1982, with France in Guadalajara (3–4) in 1986, and with Argentina in Turin (0–1) in 1990, Brazil's elimination not only lowered the flag, silenced the tambourines, and wiped away the smiles of the Brazilian girls, but also provoked many suicides in the homeland. Passion degenerated into tragedy.

In soccer joy is too often transformed into tragedy. The excess of the fans can become blood and death in the stadiums. The 1980s were marked by at least two serious disasters whose resonance was amplified by television images: Nobody can forget the scenes of the 39 fans killed at Heysel Stadium in Brussels. On May 29, 1985, the European Champions Cup Final between Juventus and Liverpool was about to begin. At one end of the field drunken English fans—"hooligans"—stampeded the Italian fans. A retaining wall crumbled and 39 were crushed by one another and buried by the debris. More than 100 were injured. The epilogue was equally paralyzing: The captains of the teams were forced to talk over the loudspeakers to calm the fans and to ask them to allow the game to be played in the hope of diminishing further provocation. English teams were suspended from the European cups for five years, but after the broadcast of the images on Eurovision soccer will never be the same.

"When you walk through the storm, hold your head up high . . .

Walk on, Walk on, with hope in your heart . . .

. . . And you'll never walk alone."

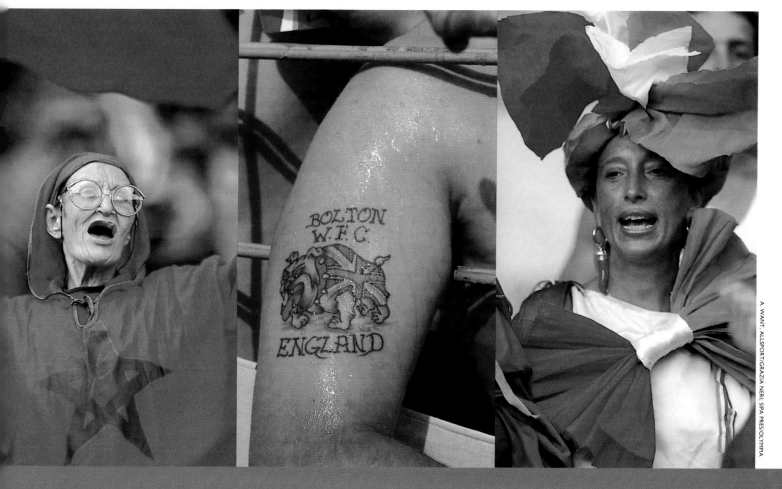

—English soccer fans' traditional victory hymn

Even worse was a tragedy in Sheffield, England, on April 15, 1989, just a few moments before the beginning of the semifinal of the F. A. Cup between Liverpool (again, what a sad coincidence) and Nottingham Forest. The police opened a gate that was weighed down by fans without tickets, but the corresponding section was already filled beyond capacity. A calamity ensued: 95 dead and 180 injured. Photos of children with their faces crushed against the railings were seen all over the world.

In the history of soccer many worse episodes have been verified. In 1964 in Lima, Peru, a clash between fans and police ended with 320 deaths. On October 20, 1982, in Moscow, a balustrade collapsed right after the 90-minute mark of a game between Spartak and Haarlem in the UEFA Cup, leaving 72 dead and 150 injured. But ten years later *Sovietski sports* revealed that there were really 340 dead—the highest death count at a soccer game in history. The images that came on May 11, 1985, from Bradford, England, made people shudder. A fire literally devoured the wooden platforms of the small, outdated stadium. In 1992 in Bastia, Corsica, during the semifinal of the French Cup, another grave disaster occurred due to a faulty setup structure: 52 dead and 200 injured. The oldest tragedy on record occurred in 1902 in Glasgow, Scotland, when a platform collapsed, leaving 25 dead and 500 injured. This, very simply, is when soccer is not the most beautiful game in the world.

"That's a bloody cup."

— Taunting graffiti written by fans of Juventus's local rival, Torino, in Turin after Heysel tragedy

Soccer's worst hooliganism incident: 39 people died in Heysel Stadium, Brussels, after Liverpool fans stampeded Juventus supporters at the 1985 European Champions Cup Final.

Astar shone over soccer in the 1980s: Diego Armando Maradona. Of his talents only one thing can be said: He is the heir to Pelé. Some have even thought him to be superior. But his miseries have been as dramatic as his successes. The career of the Argentine is unique in every way: three times a player in the World Cup finals, and a fourth tournament coming; a world title in Mexico; triumphs in South America for country and club and in Europe for Barcelona and Napoli. On the other hand, he has been arrested in a drug-induced delirium and faced with trials, fines, disqualifications, an illegitimate son, physical degeneration, and bad friendships. All this—and still an incredible rebirth in 1993.

Maradona was born on October 30, 1960, in Lanús, the fifth son of a poor family. As a child he moved to Buenos Aires. The soccer ball became his most faithful friend—his cousin Beto gave him his first. In the streets of Barrio Fiorito, on the outskirts of Buenos Aires, the swarthy *peluso* put on a show. Argentinos Juniors signed him as a professional on December 8, 1973: Diego was 13 years old. Evita Perón attended the final game of the season, in which Argentinos beat Rio Plata 5–4 with two goals scored by Diego. His ascent was then unstoppable. On February 27, 1977, Maradona made his first appearance in the national team; at 16 years and 4 months old, he was younger than Pelé was in his first national appearance. He played for 65 minutes in a match against Hungary, which was won by Argentina, 4–0.

His first disappointment came in May 1978: Coach Cesar Luis Menotti excluded Maradona from the world championship team because he was too inexperienced. But Diego got even the following year, leading Argentina to the world youth championship title in Tokyo. Pelé noticed him then and warned, "Accept the applause but don't live only for it." From that moment on, Maradona raced from one triumph to the next: best player in South America, top scorer for Argentina, a world-record transfer fee in 1979 to Boca Juniors ($1.5 million). As *El Grafico* had written, "Maradona is soccer." In 1981 Boca Juniors won the Argentine championship. Barcelona then bought his contract for $5 million (another world-record fee). In the 1982 World Cup finals in Spain, Diego reacted rashly to the physical abuse of defenders and the misguided attentions of the press. At the end of the year, in Barcelona, he suffered from hepatitis and was laid up for three months. The next year was even worse: Real Madrid's Julio Andoni Goicoechea broke Maradona's left ankle in one of the typically brutal tackles he so often suffered.

Maradona preferred to leave Spain, and Napoli president Corrado Ferlaino bought him in 1984 for yet another world-record fee ($8 million). On July 5, at Napoli's San Paolo Stadium, sixty thousand fans came to see his first training session. The mature Maradona now was known to frequent undesirable places in Naples. He actually trained very little. But Napoli and the Neapolitans excused him because they were sure he was stronger on the field than elsewhere in life. In 1986, at the World Cup finals in Mexico, Maradona practically won the tournament by himself. "Maradona and ten to be named" was Carlos Bilardo's description of his team. Diego was invincible, thanks to the enforced regime of Bilardo, who kept him in camp for six weeks. No excesses—just training. He was then qualified to be the second Pelé.

Preceding pages: Maradona in the lineup at the 1990 World Cup. Left: Maradona challenging the Belgian defense in the 1982 World Cup. Below: Maradona in 1986.

Maradona

Argentina's "Pibe de Oro"

"No, I am never satisfied: Now I must have the *Italian* title."

Maradona to the Italian press corps after winning the 1986 World Cup

The world title gave him new courage. In 1987, a few months after the birth of his first daughter, Djalmita, he celebrated his first Italian league (Serie A) title with Napoli. But Maradona then became more polemical with the club, Ferlaino, and the fans. He fluctuated between wanting to leave and staying; occasionally he actually fled to Buenos Aires. The problems with his coach, Ottavio Bianchi, became impossible. Scandals erupted in his private life: A woman from Naples, Cristiana Sinagra, forced a paternity suit. The case dragged on for years. Diego refused to take blood tests, but it was his son and he had to pay child support. Compromising photographs were released of Diego with members of the Camorra. But in sports, success can mean everything, and in 1989 Napoli won its first UEFA Cup. In 1990 he celebrated winning another Serie A title. But Maradona's relationship with the public turned sour when the Procura of Naples released a dossier of his legal troubles.

At Italia '90 he showcased his talents, but the crowd jeered him. In Naples, Argentina eliminated Italy in the semifinal and Maradona was triumphant—but losing the final, he spent the last minutes of the game weeping. He fled to South America and was later arrested there in an apparent state of confusion, high on cocaine. He was overweight because he hadn't been training, although maintaining his ideal weight had always been a problem.

But . . . he was still Maradona, and FIFA invested in his return to World Cup 1994. General Secretary Joseph S. Blatter administered his passage to Seville with a minimum of controversy, and in 1992 Diego returned to the field after the obligatory international suspension for drugs. He faced a tough season but regained his confidence on the ball. Then, with disappointing predictability, he fought with Seville and returned to Argentina. After a silence, a new Maradona reappeared: seventeen kilos lighter and far from drugs. Newell's Old Boys signed him, and the Argentine coach, Alfio Basile, called him up for the play-offs with Australia to determine the last place for World Cup 1994. Diego played; Argentina qualified. *Plus ça change.*

1986 World Cup Final: Maradona overcomes West Germany's Karl-Heinz Foerster and goalkeeper Harald Schumacher for Argentina's second goal, and holds up the FIFA trophy.

Although United States international soccer history dates to November 28, 1885, when a U.S. team was defeated by Canada 1–0 in Newark, New Jersey, the Stars-and-Stripes team has never been a world power. Not in the 1930s, when, taking part in the first World Cup in Uruguay, the team succeeded in beating Belgium and Paraguay (both by 3–0) before yielding 1–6 to that World Cup's second-place team, Argentina. Nor in the postwar period—although one flickering moment, a 1–0 victory over England at Belo Horizonte during the 1950 World Cup finals, is one of soccer's historic moments. If there were some encouraging showings in the U.S. Cups of 1992 and 1993, much is owed to one of three brothers who played for Belgrade's Partizan club in the 1960s: Bora Milutinović. After six seasons as midfielder, four Yugoslavian titles, and one cup with Partizan, he emigrated to France (because of Yugoslavian soccer federation rules he

Team USA

could not leave the country until age 28), where he played for Monaco, Nice, Rouen, and then the Swiss team, Winterthur. From there, Bora moved to Mexico, where he married Mari Carmen (they have a daughter, Darinka) and started his career as a coach. He spent twelve seasons with the Pumas at the Universidad Autonoma de Mexico, the first three still as a player and the rest as their full-time coach.

Milutinović is keenly perceptive yet romantic—as well as lucky—but mostly a talented professional. From Bajina Bašta in Serbia, where he was born fifty-four years ago, he came to the United States in March 1991 and lives in Laguna Miguel, California. With his fringe of hair always falling over his black eyebrows and his penchant for taking risks, he has an air of eternal youth.

He first appeared at the 1986 World Cup in Mexico. He coached the home team well; they were eliminated only by West Germany in the quarterfinals after overtime. He was present four years later at the World Cup in Italy, in charge of the team from Costa Rica, which surprisingly made it to the second round.

Cobi Jones (far right) leads the 1993 United States national team near the Mission Viejo training camp. Team USA's 1993 record included a 2–0 victory over England and participation in the Copa America.

Right: Coach of the U.S. national team since 1991, Bora Milutinović, in training camp. Opposite: Forward Thomas Dooley (formerly Kaiserslautern; now Team USA) vs. Italy, U.S. Cup, 1992.

The Bora Connection

Bora Milutinović's third, and most difficult, wager began on March 27, 1991. This time, his task was greater because of the lack of an American soccer tradition, both at a psychological and at a technical level. "The main problem," Milutinović has explained, "is preparation, because among the twenty-four countries which will be represented at the World Cup, the United States is the only one which does not have a regular championship, so I don't have any reference points. And it makes me laugh when I hear that Italy's Sacchi is able to see two club games in one day: one in the afternoon and another at night." In order to make the national team worthy of its name, Milutinović followed the examples set by Arrigo Sacchi, whom he admires greatly, and Silvio Berlusconi in Milan.

Only after receiving suitable guarantees for his proposals did Milutinović sign a contract with the United States Soccer Federation. He prearranged a long training period of seventeen months before the World Cup; he chose the training site in Mission Viejo; and he was able to select a group of thirty players, most fresh out of university, who have made their homes in the surrounding area in exchange for salaries varying between $1,200 and $4,100 per month and the distant prospect of becoming famous in the future. None of them, including Milutinović, is well known in the United States. More than once in American soccer circles Milutinović has had to introduce himself.

"Nobody knows who we are," Milutinović says with a smile, "but I have young men following me with great passion. We train Monday through Saturday, and three times a week we train three times a day: Tuesdays, Thursdays, and Fridays." Training, training, training, and many lessons on theory, tactics, and sense. "I like to talk to the hearts of these young men," explains Milutinović, "and it is often more important to make them laugh than sweat."

Between training and laughing there is room to play games all over the world. In 1993 the United States team played 34 international matches with 10 wins, 13 losses, and 11 ties. But what matters most is bringing the team together for the final sprint, when Milutinović is counting on gathering together the rest of his players, who are presently scattered all over Europe. Among the best are Roy Wegerle, who plays for Coventry City in England; Eric Wynalda, who plays for F.C. Saarbrucken in Germany; Ernie Stewart, who plays for Willem in Holland; Frank Klopas, who played for AEK Athens in Greece; John Harkes, who plays for Derby County in England; Tab Ramos (from Uruguay), who plays for Betis Seville in Spain; and the defender John Doyle, who plays for VfB Leipzig in Germany.

"As strange as it may sound," added Milutinović, "they earn much more in Europe than in America, and I, having been all over the world, can't criticize them." The coach's complete team will be together only one month before the World Cup. Yet it will be difficult, even for him, to leave out someone who has sacrificed six days a week for a year and a half. "We know that we won't be able to go far," concludes Milutinović, "but we also know we play an important role. At the World Cup in Italy, the United States only lost to Italy 0–1. No, we're not hoping to tie Italy. It would be enough only if we beat them in the first round. It is important to show that Bora is still Bora." Ready for a new assignment—no matter where.

Former University of Virginia teammates and current members of the national side.
Below left: midfielder John Harkes (who plays for Derby County in England).
Below right: goalkeeper Tony Meola (Team USA).

finalist. The Cameroonians were beaten by two penalties. Their captain, Roger Milla, 38 years old at that time and on reprieve from retirement, was among the the cup's top scorers, with four goals, and was the absolute star of the tournament.

The difficulty for African soccer is to fill the technical and organizational gap that separates it from European soccer. The best African players are still compelled to emigrate, and this greatly penalizes the level of soccer and the national teams. In this way, talented young players who have remained in their homelands miss out on professional championships that would complete their maturation. Of the thirty-seven African federations that signed up for the qualifications for the 1994 World Cup; many were forced to pull out for lack of funds. This will be the first World Cup in which Africa will have a third finalist. With Morocco and Cameroon to represent the tradition (the only two countries from the continent that can boast of participating three times), there will also be, for the first time, Nigeria, the most populated country in Africa (with more than 100 million people). Of course, considering how Africans fared in the latest editions, it still seems that there is a disproportion between Africa's 3 places in the final phase compared with the 3.5 for South America (10 national teams competed for World Cup 1994) and the 13 for Europe (36 national teams competed for World Cup 1994). But one thing is certain: If Africans do well in USA 1994, there will be absolutely no need to speak any more of surprises.

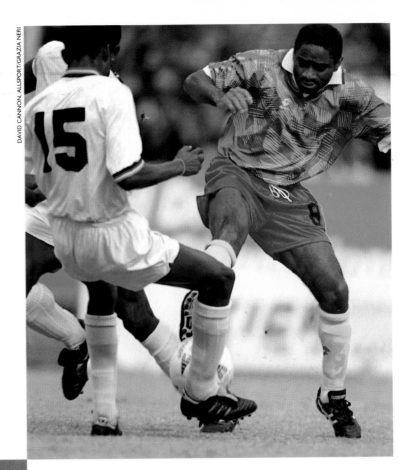

DAVID CANNON, ALLSPORT/GRAZIA NERI

. . .That time is now, folks."

Cameroon's Emile M'bouh, 1994 World Cup qualifying match vs. Zimbabwe. Below: Congo's Laurent Nsomi.

Below: Nigeria's Thompson Oliha, 1994 African World Cup qualifier.

–Cameroon's Roger Milla, 1990 World Cup

NEAL SIMPSON, BOB THOMAS/EMPICS/RICHIARDI

NEAL SIMPSON, BOB THOMAS/EMPICS/RICHIARDI

The Players
and
The Game

SORIANO TEMP SPORT/RICHIARDI

Brazil's and Barcelona's Romario (right) vs. São Paulo

**"Football is a simple game made
difficult by the players."**

**Attributed to Arthur Rowse,
Ken Jones, *The Independent*, November 18, 1993**

"Until now I have only won coffee-shop tournaments; now is the time to get serious."
Roberto Baggio, 1993 UEFA Cup Final

Left: Italy's and Juventus's forward and 1993 FIFA Player of the Year, Roberto Baggio: a Buddhist, he often wears an armband with a hand-written Hindi aphorism, roughly translatable as "we must win."

Tassos Mitropoulos of Greece (left) and Florian Urban of Hungary in qualifying game for the 1994 World Cup. Left: Switzerland's and Zurich Grasshopper's midfielder Alain Sutter in qualifying victory for the 1994 World Cup (1–0) over Italy.

Following pages: Holland's and Inter Milan's deep-lying forward Dennis Bergkamp passes Denmark's John Sievebaek and Eric Larsen in the 1992 European Championships.

Barcelona's and Spain's forward Julio Salinas helped to revive Spain in the 1994 World Cup qualifying rounds.

Bulgaria's striker Hristo Stoichkov (left) won a European Cup medal with Barcelona in 1992. Right: Germany's and Bayern Munich's 1991 FIFA Player of the Year, Lothar Matthäus is perhaps the world's finest playmaker.

Brazil's Zico perfected the art in 1986. Below: Italy's and A.C. Milan's forward Gianluigi Lentini.

Bicycle kicks

Olympic Marseilles's Eric Di Meco, 1993 European Cup Final vs. A.C. Milan.

Fouls

1993's most notorious foul: Holland's Ronald Koeman. . .

. . .pulls down England's David Platt as they cross into. . .

Denmark's and Barcelona's Michael Laudrup is felled in a Spanish Premier League match.

. . .the Dutch penalty area. Koeman was cautioned, no penalty. . .

. . .was given, in the critical World Cup qualifying game.

Sweden's Jan Eriksson is attended to by Germany's Matthias Sammer, 1992 European Championships.

"Your father is only trying to become a man."

Opposite above: Denmark's Henrik Andersen; Opposite below: Ireland's Tommy Coyne and Switzerland's Peter Schepull, in an international "friendly" (exhibition) match; Left: Belarus referee cautioning player, Brussels vs. Anderlecht, 1993 European Cup; Below: Russia's and Olympique Marseilles's Igor Dobrovolski is ordered to play on. Page 120: France and A.C. Milan's Jean-Pierre Papin collides with national teammate Basile Boli of Olympique Marseilles; Page 121: Marseilles's Franck Sauzée tackled by Milan's captain, Franco Baresi, and Paolo Maldini and Demetrio Albertini in the 1993 European Cup Final.

OLYMPIA

SHAUN BOTTERILL, ALLSPORT/GRAZIA NERI

Opposite: 1992 FIFA World Player of the Year: Holland's and A.C. Milan's Marco Van Basten. Below: Brazil's and Deportivo La Coruña's Bebeto, 1989 South American Player of the Year and top scorer (29 goals) in 1993 Spanish Premier League.

Preceding pages: Sweden's and Parma's Tomas Brolin (center) shoots past Denmark's Lars Olsen in the 1992 European Championships.

Right: Romania's and Brescia's midfield playmaker, Gheorghe Hagi. Below: Germany's and Borussia Dortmund's goal-scoring Karl-Heinz Riedle in the 1992 European Championships.

> "Climate, temperament, history—all these contribute to style, which is an aspect of character, individual or national."

Official Football Association Yearbook, 1963

Colombia's and Junior Barranquilla's Carlos Valderrama receives a Uruguayan tackle, 1993 Copa America. Following pages: The Dutch Wall, 1992 European Championships.

BOB THOMAS/RICHIARDI

Aston Villa F.C.

England: National Team

Walls

USSR: National Team (1990)

Tottenha

Mexico: National Team

North Korea: National Team

otspur F.C.

Brazil: National Team

France: National Team

"This is the happiest day of my life—and I am not on a soccer field."

Ruud Gullit, active campaigner against racial segregation, after Nelson Mandela's release from a South African prison in 1990

RICHIARDI

Left: Holland's and Sampdoria's Ruud Gullit (shown here with A.C. Milan; Gullit was transferred to Sampdoria in the summer of 1993). Right: Russia's and Foggia's center forward, Igor Kolivanov. Following pages: Brazil's Renato Portaluppi shoots toward England's Tony Dorigo, Martin Keown, and goalkeeper Chris Woods in a 1992 international friendly.

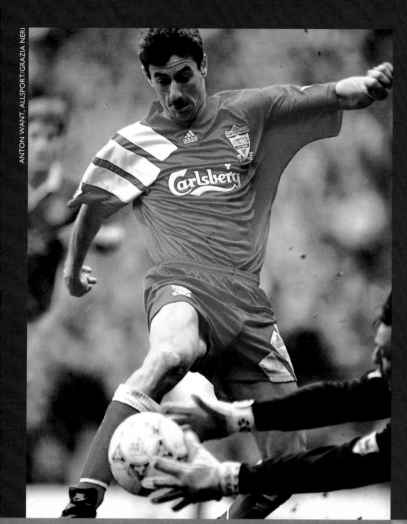

ANTON WANT, ALLSPORT/GRAZIA NERI

The Great Club Rivalries

"It is the second rule of football (the first being that the ref is always biased against your team) that to be a true fan you must hate your nearest local rivals."

Polly Nicolson, Newcastle, England; Letter to *The Independent on Sunday*, October 31, 1993

OLYMPIA

Left: Glasgow Celtic vs. Glasgow Rangers: Richard Gough and Mark Hateley of Rangers sandwich a Celtic player in the "Old Firm" rivalry; Celtic and Rangers first met in 1890.
Above: Everton's goalie Neville Southall and Liverpool's Ian Rush in a game from the 100-year-old "Merseyside derby."
Right: A.C. Milan vs. Internazionale Milan: Milan's Franco Baresi clashes with Inter's Aldo Serena. Milan's two teams have played each other 226 times since 1908.

OLYMPIA

• GOL • BUT • TÖR • DOEL • GOAL • MÅL • GOL • BUT • TÖR • DOEL • GO

• DOEL • GOAL • MÅL • GOL • BUT • TÖR • DOEL • GOAL • GOL • TÖR • DO

• GOL • BUT • TÖR • DOEL • GOAL • MÅL • GOL • BUT • TÖR • DOEL • GO

• DOEL • GOAL • MÅL • GOL • BUT • TÖR • DOEL • GOAL • GOL • TÖR • DO

• GOL • BUT • TÖR • DOEL • GOAL • MÅL • GOL • BUT • TÖR • DOEL • GO

• DOEL • GOAL • MÅL • GOL • BUT • TÖR • DOEL • GOAL • GOL • TÖR • DO

• GOL • BUT • TÖR • DOEL • GOAL • MÅL • GOL • BUT • TÖR • DOEL • GO

• DOEL • GOAL • MÅL • GOL • BUT • TÖR • DOEL • GOAL • GOL • TÖR • DO

• GOL • BUT • TÖR • DOEL • GOAL • MÅL • GOL • BUT • TÖR • DOEL • GO

• DOEL • GOAL • MÅL • GOL • BUT • TÖR • DOEL • GOAL • GOL • TÖR • DO

JOHN MCDERMOTT

Germany's Lothar Matthäus, 1993 U.S. Cup.

"Chest—Foot—IN!" —Alan McLoughlin, describing his goal that put

GOAL • TÖR • DOEL • GOL GOAL • DOEL MÅL • GOL BUT • TÖR • DOEL GOL DOEL •
TÖR • MÅL • GOL • BUT • TÖR • TÖR • DOEL • GOAL • GOL • BUT • TÖR DOEL •
GOAL • TÖR • DOEL • GOAL • GOL • GÅL • GOL • BUT • TÖR • DOEL • GOAL •
GOL • MÅL • GOL • BUT • TÖR • DOEL • GOAL • GOL • BUT • TÖR GOL DOEL •
GOAL • TÖR • DOEL • GOAL • MÅL • GOL BUT • TÖR • DOEL GOAL •
GOL • MÅL • GOL • BUT • TÖR • DOEL • GOAL • GOL • BUT • TÖR • DOEL •
GOAL • TÖR • DOEL • GOAL • MÅL • GOL BUT • TÖR • DOEL GOAL •
MÅL • GOL • BUT • TÖR • DOEL • GOAL • GOL • BUT • TÖR • DOEL •
GOAL • TÖR • DOEL • GOAL • MÅL • GOL • BUT • TÖR • DOEL • GOAL •

...reland in the 1994 World Cup; *The New York Times*, November 18, 1993

Top: Argentina scores vs. Bulgaria, 1990 World Cup. Middle row: penalty shoot-outs: Arsenal's Seaman saves vs. Manchester United's Irwin; Argentina's Goycoechea, 1990 World Cup vs. Italy; Middle right: Juventus's Baggio scores vs. Bologna; Bottom row: Denmark's Schmeichel saves vs. Holland's Van Basten, 1992 semifinal European Championships.

"I learned that the ball never came to you where you expected it. Thi

helped me in life." Albert Camus, philosopher and goalkeeper, "Football in Algiers," *France Football,* 1957

Top row: Denmark's and Manchester United's Peter Schmeichel; Saudi Arabia's Samar Alotaibi; Mexico's and Universidad of America's Jorge Campos, who has also played forward—and led the Mexican league in scoring.

I,328 goals have been scored in 412 World

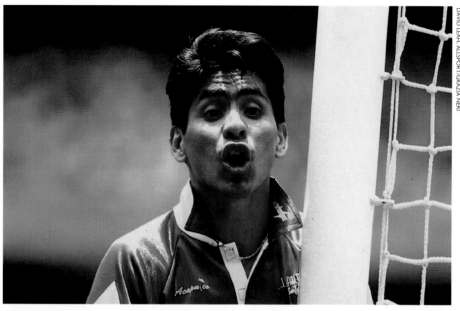

DAVID LEAH, ALLSPORT/GRAZIA NERI

FRESCO, RICHIARDI

Far left: Spain's and Barcelona's Andoni Zubi- zarreta, quali- fying match vs. Denmark for 1994 World Cup Left: The World Cup's most scored- against goal- keeper, full- time bus dri- ver Pier Luigi Benedettini of San Marino, vs. England, 1994 World Cup qualifier.

Cup finals matches, from 1930 to 1990

Republic of Ireland's and Manchester United's Roy Keane in action against Northern Ireland, 1994 World Cup qualifying match. Left: Republic of Ireland's and Aston Villa's Andy Townsend, 1994 World Cup qualifying match vs. Lithuania.

Belgium and Monaco's midfielder Enzo Scifo (shown here playing for Torino).

First in the nation, second best at home? In this age of club teams composed of an international medley of players, forward Pier Luigi Casiraghi has found himself unable to make either Juventus's or Lazio's starting teams, although he holds a regular place in the national team. Casiraghi is not alone: A.C. Milan's reserves are stocked with international stars. 1993 international friendly vs. Germany.

RICHIARDI

Saudi Arabia's Fahad Mehalel breaches the South Korean defense, 1994 World Cup qualifiers (final round).

Iraq's Ahmad Radhi hurdles Iran's Janed Zarine in their first World Cup meeting since the Iran–Iraq war.

"Never before in the history of
any official qualifying tournament do
we have 16 of such diverse political
and ideological backgrounds."

Peter Velappan, FIFA, 1994 World Cup
Asian qualifying tournament,
The Sunday Telegraph, October 17, 1993

"The politics of soccer
can sometimes be even harder than
the politics of the Middle East."

Dr. Henry Kissinger, October 1991

APL PHOTOSPORT, ALLSPORT/GRAZIA NERI

Australia's and Adelaide City's Carl Veart in the 1994 World Cup Oceania qualifiers, vs. New Zealand.

San Marino—the team from the World Cup's smallest
country (38 square miles; population: 20,000).

Wales's and Manchester United's teenage star Ryan Giggs,
in a gesture symbolic of Great Britain's despair as all four
teams failed to make the 1994 World Cup finals.

Celebration!

Above left: Norway's
Goran Sorloth, vs.
England, 1994 World
Cup qualifier.
Left: Argentina's
and Fiorentina's
Gabriel
Batistuta,
vs. Mexico,
1993 Copa
America
Final.

SHAUN BOTTERILL, ALSPORT/GRAZIA NERI

DAN SMITH, ALSPORT/GRAZIA NERI

Above: Colombia's and Parma's Faustino Asprilla. Above right: Mexico's and Rayo Vallecano's Hugo Sanchez. Right: Bolivia's forward Marco Antonio Etcheverry, vs. Venezuela, 1993.

RICHIARDI

DAVID LEAH ALLSPORT/GRAZIA NERI

**Above: Mexico during its 1994
World Cup qualifying victory over
El Salvador. Preceding pages:
Denmark celebrates winning the
1992 European Championships in
2–1 victory over Germany.**

"One shuddering heap of ecstati

umanity." Nick Hornby, *Fever Pitch*, 1992

**Argentina celebrates goal in 1994
World Cup qualifier vs. Australia.
Left: Germany's triumphant pairs:
Klinsmann and Littbarski, Buchwald
and Vöeller (and Matthäus, no.10),
1990 World Cup.**

As the United States looks forward to World Cup 1994, hosting the largest event in the history of soccer, no one expects the Americans to win against so many technically superior teams. But in the United States there *is* a national soccer team that has already won a world competition, the current title holder. The only American soccer team ever to win an international tournament is the women's soccer team, victors in the first FIFA Women's World Championships in 1991 in China. Theirs was a triumphant path as they beat Sweden, Brazil, Japan, Taiwan, Germany, and, in the final, Norway.

Women's style of play varies regionally, and the women's championship reflected these differences: The Scandinavians rely on great athletic ability; Germany and Italy play physical soccer; the Chinese display quickness and precision; and the Americans are known for their physical prowess and aggressiveness. Women's soccer concentrates on strategy and tactics: Fairer and with fewer fouls, it is a passing game that emphasizes skill and technique rather than pace and stamina.

The modern women's soccer movement began almost twenty years ago in the United States and Europe, preceded by sporadic local initiatives dating back to the 1920s. National and world soccer organizations had long maintained that women either had no interest or no place in soccer. Southern Europe in particular rejected women's soccer, smothered by the overpowering demand for men's soccer and by biases against women in athletics. For years the mass media mistakenly assumed from syndicated reports that the few young women in soccer were boys, masculinizing their names. Arguments that physical exertion could be damaging to women's anatomy, prevalent in the first half of this century, are still heard in various forms: It was only in 1990 that the England Schools Football Association was allowed to "actively encourage" soccer for girls. The first women's matches were played to audiences who attended out of prurience, curiosity, and incredulity. At the Seven Sisters schools on the East Coast, women began to play soccer in the 1920s. The players would practice as teams at their respective schools and then would converge for games. These events, called "Playdays," did not pit one school team against another, because competition was thought to be a corruptive force, the women would randomly mingle into combined teams. Today, the United States and China continue to draw national players from their scholastic reserves, in contrast to Europe's and Japan's small but established networks of professional and semiprofessional leagues.

Unlike American men who fall behind for lack of soccer history, women began seriously playing the game in the United States at the same time as the rest of the world, in the late 1960s and early 1970s, making them internationally competitive.

Players

Women

Kristine Lilly, undefeated UNC player and U.S. NCAA champion, in a 1993 World Student Games match vs. Japan.

Sweden vs. Norway, semifinal, 1991 FIFA WWC (1–4). Many American athletes play for European sides: Akers-Stahl plays for a division one Swedish team, but would like an American league so that "I don't have to go over there to get games."

Notes Shawn Ladda, coach of Columbia University's team, "Soccer is cultural and people feel it very deeply. That's part of why the U.S. team is so successful. It's not the macho sport of this country." In England, women's soccer has boomed over the last two years. Television coverage of the 1989 Women's Football Association Cup drew almost two million viewers. In the United Kingdom, 45,000 women play soccer; three million in the United States; 550,000 in Germany; and 27,000 in Norway. Italy has both professional and semiprofessional women's leagues, and Japan's professional league is now two years old. Girls now comprise 40 percent of American youth play and women are strongly represented in collegiate programs. In 1991, 65 out of FIFA's 151 countries had women's teams. Although progress has been slower in South America and Africa, women's soccer is gradually growing out of its preliminary stages. After much campaigning, women's soccer will be an Olympic event for the first time in 1996. Parity between men's and women's soccer is still far away: whereas the men's national team players received $3,300 per month for World Cup practice, the women earned only $1,000.

Although interest in women's soccer seems to be expanding by every available measure, it is still far more a participation sport than a spectator sport. Like women's tennis, however, it fills a particular niche: because play is slower and more tactical, it affords a certain attention to strategy and nuance. The championship in China announced the viability of the sport as the women played to full stadiums and a large television market. The event was immensely profitable, with 65,000 paying spectators at the final game and a live broadcast to millions in almost fifty nations worldwide. Despite resistance and a late arrival on the world stage, milestones like the 1995 women's championship in Stockholm and the debut in the 1996 Olympics suggest that the sport has a promising future.

—Michelle Akers-Stahl, U.S. forward and World Champion

giving up so much?"

Left: Women's collegiate soccer, North Carolina State vs. University of Virginia in an Atlantic Coast Conference game.

"How could we lose after

Germany vs. Sweden, third-place game, 1991 FIFA Women's World Championships. Following pages: The United States, in first FIFA Women's World Championships, celebrates 2–1 victory over Norway in the final, 1991.

A History of the Game's Tactics

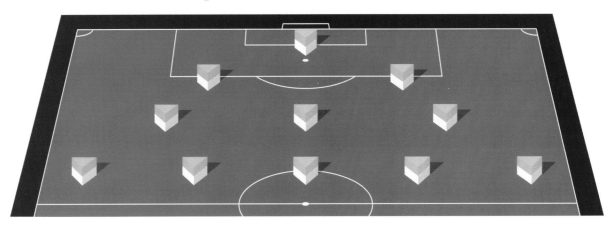

When soccer was first organized in the mid-1800s, it was assumed that the offense was the most important part of every team. So it followed that the pioneer players instinctively threw themselves together into attacks on the opponent's goal. Little by little it was understood that this approach was, in reality, a rudimentary tactic that left them too exposed to opposing counteroffensives. And so the first tactical lineup was formed, based on three lines of players in front of the goalkeeper, who was called on, as always, to guard the goal. This type of lineup, in which players kept to their linear positions, consisted of two fullbacks, three halfbacks, and five forwards. The center half (the central midfielder) marked the opposing center forward and was both the key playmaker and the pivot between the defense and the offense. Seen from above, this lineup appears to be a pyramid, with the goalkeeper at the top and the five forwards at the bottom. Because of the English roots of the game, the names of the positions—goalkeeper, fullback, halfback, wing (or winger), and forward—took root in many parts of the world in English. Changes in soccer strategy evolved slowly from the origins of soccer in the late nineteenth century until the threshold of the First World War (1914–1918).

The Method, or MM

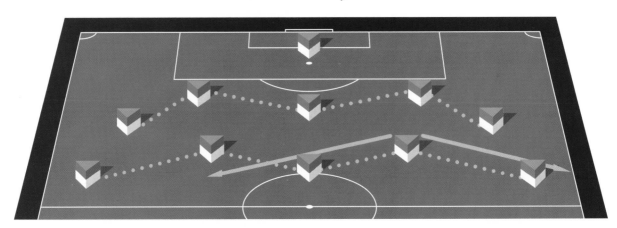

It was not until after World War I that soccer strategy started to undergo a distinct metamorphosis: in Europe the "Method," or MM, came into fashion. (The British, playing the game in isolation, practiced a different game plan with closer marking of opponents.) Two backs and two wing halfbacks lined up with a center half to delineate the first, more withdrawn "M" in front of the goalkeeper. The two wing halves on either side of the three forwards formed the second, more advanced "M." With the Method, Uruguay (1930 and 1950) and Italy (1934 and 1938) won the World Cup, thanks not only to the talents of individual players but especially to teamwork. The Method was practiced by the famous Austrian "Wunderteam," which was considered by the experts to be the best European soccer team outside of Britain in the 1930s. The Austrian teams moved in a linear fashion, using short passes played across the lines of the "M"s to keep possession of the ball.

The System, or WM

After World War II the "System," also known as WM, was developed to counter the strengths of the Method. Anticipated by the British in the 1930s, the System was really a variation of the Method. In front of the goalkeeper there were now three defenders—the center half of the Method becoming a defender—spread across the field on the same line. In the midfield, two halfbacks and two wing halves formed a "quadrilateral," and three forwards were aligned up front. Although the

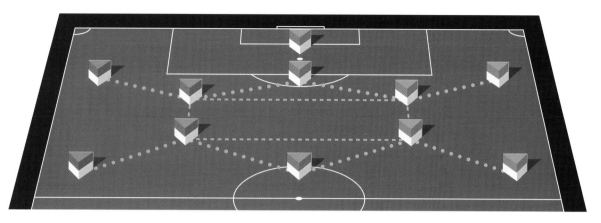

System gained much popularity and was used everywhere, Uruguay won the 1950 World Cup using the Method, now characterized by a player roaming diagonally across the field (plate 2) and capable of anything, especially of starting attacks from turnovers. For Uruguay that player was Schiaffino, the first great wing half playmaker.

The Honved Model

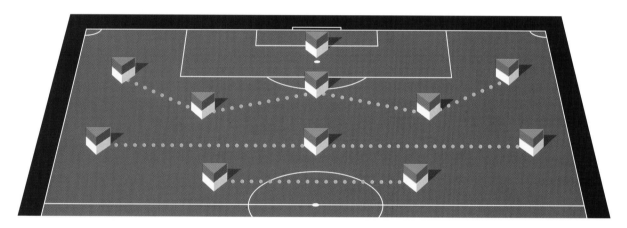

The Hungarian club Honved F.C., from Budapest, made an indelible mark in the beginning of the 1950s. The great Hungarian national teams took most of their players from this club team. Similar to the MM and WM designations, the Honved Model, attributed to Gustav Sebes, vice minister of sport and coach of the national team, could be called WW. The defending line and the midfield line remain the same as in the System, but the forward line is reversed. The wings and the center forward are behind the inside forwards (the System's wing halfs), who now play in a more forward role than in the System. Wings and center forward provide the front line of forwards, rather than the reverse.

For the Honved team, Kocsis and Puskas played up front, whereas the wings, Budai and Czibor, withdrew to the same line as the now withdrawn center forward, Hidegkuti, the first celebrated player who was able to use this deep-lying position to take defenders by surprise.

From the Sweeping Game to the *Libero*

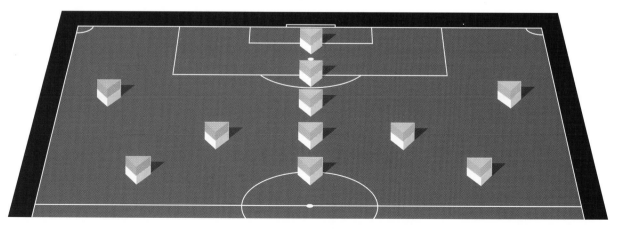

The 1950s saw the introduction of the epoch of excessive defense—best described as, "First, don't let in a goal, then take the enemy by surprise via the center forward." Although such play was not spectacular, it was often profitable for the Swiss national team and the Swiss club Servette Geneva, both coached by the Austrian Karl Rappan, who gave the name of this scheme to history: *verrou* in Swiss-German (*béton* in French, *catenaccio* in Italian, literally "bolt" in English). It was first practiced in Italy by Padova in 1941, and became popular in the 1950s. The marking of the opponents was tight—man to man—sometimes with help from an overlapping winger who could defend or move forward. But in the long run, this scheme did not pay off, and after the 1950s it was modified because of the need

for better defense. There was always the risk that the center half, in line with the two backs, might be isolated in front of the opposing forwards: once past him, in fact, the center forward came face to face with the goalkeeper and therefore was in the best situation to score a goal. To prevent this, a *libero*—the free man or "sweeper"—was necessary in front of the goalkeeper and behind the backs and center half, who in this scheme still marked the center forward and became the "stopper," in soccer terminology. The idea was to offer additional security to the defense.

The sweeper formation has been popular among professional teams in most countries for decades, and the last three World Cups were won by teams playing in this formation: Italy in 1982 with Gaetano Scirea as sweeper; Argentina in 1986 with José-Luis Brown; and Germany in 1990 with Klaus Augenthaler. Franz Beckenbauer, who won the World Cup as a player in 1974, revolutionized the role in the 1970s by turning it into a position from which, when free of defensive responsibilities, attacks could first be mounted.

By Man—By Zone

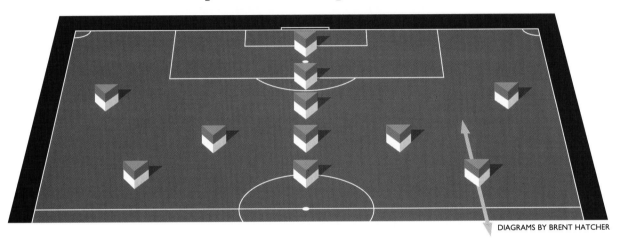

DIAGRAMS BY BRENT HATCHER

Recently, soccer tactics have undergone changes, often very shortlived, but the contrast between zone play and man-to-man play remains. The first change is a derivation of the Method, in which players are marked according to their position on the field and schemes are determined by the behavior of the opponent. Specific man-to-man markings are not used. There are two peculiar characteristics of zone play: the full press and the offside trap. Zone play takes a scientific approach to the offside trap; when the opponent attacks, the defense moves up, causing the opponents to withdraw or risk being offside, as well as cutting

off the opposing forwards. This means that the defensive phase begins practically at the same moment in which control of the ball is lost. Pressing—an aggressive attempt to move forward and control the opponent in possession of the ball—immediately takes place.

Most teams are now starting to play the zone system, and from experience most coaches maintain that the 4-4-2 arrangement is the most functional and profitable: four defenders in line (or almost), four midfielders in line (or almost), and two forwards. The most common variations are 4-3-3, with one

midfielder becoming a forward or a winger who tries to spread the defense, or 4-2-4. But other schemes exist, the most effective of which was used a great deal in the 1990 World Cup in Italy, although the first to use it were the Belgian clubs Anderlecht and Malines. This scheme foresaw the sweeper behind or on line with the four defenders in the so-called "five-man defense," which was also used at Italia '90 by England, Germany, and Brazil. But three defenders can also play by zone with the sweeper behind, as shown by the 1990 Soviet team of Valeri Lobanovski.

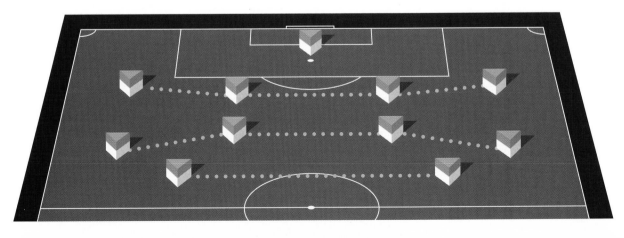

World Cup and National Statistics

Overall World Cup Statistics

	1930	1934	1938	1950	1954	1958	1962	1966	1970	1974	1978	1982	1986	1990	1994
Registered Nations	13	32	36	32	38	51	56	81	70	99	106	108	121	112	145
Nations in Qualifying Tournament	0	29	32	27	36	48	51	53	70	92	98	105	113	105	130
Nations in Finals	13	16	15	13	16	16	16	16	16	16	16	24	24	24	24
Venue	Uruguay	Italy	France	Brazil	Switzerland	Sweden	Chile	England	Mexico	Germany	Argentina	Spain	Mexico	Italy	USA
Matches Played in Finals	18	17	18	22	26	35	32	32	32	38	38	52	52	52	52
Total Players in Finals	189	208	210	192	233	241	252	254	270	264	277	396	414	413	
Goals Scored	70	70	84	88	140	126	89	89	95	97	102	146	132	115	
Team Goal Average	3.8	4.1	4.7	4	5.3	3.9	2.8	2.8	3	2.6	2.7	2.8	2.5	2.2	
Penalties Awarded	2	4	3	3	7	8	8	8	4	8	14	10	16	18	
Penalties Scored	1	3	2	3	7	7	8	8	4	6	12	8	12	13	
Total Attendance	434,500	395,000	483,000	1,337,000	943,000	868,000	776,000	1,614,677	1,673,975	1,774,022	1,610,215	1,856,277	2,402,951	2,517,348	
Average Game Attendance	24,138	23,235	26,833	60,772	36,270	24,800	24,250	50,458	52,311	46,684	42,374	33,967	46,211	48,411	

World Cup Qualifying Tournaments Team Records: 1930–1994

OCEANIA

	Points	Played	Won	Lost	Tied	Goals For	Goals Against
Australia*	80	64	30	20	14	126	62
New Zealand	50	44	19	12	13	102	51
Fiji	12	14	4	4	6	14	43
Tahiti	3	4	1	1	2	5	8
Solomon Islands	1	4	0	1	3	5	13
Vanuatu	0	4	0	0	4	1	18

SOUTH AMERICA

	Points	Played	Won	Lost	Tied	Goals For	Goals Against
Brazil	66	38	29	8	1	100	14
Uruguay	58	42	24	10	8	61	34
Paraguay	52	50	20	12	18	68	57
Argentina	46	32	20	6	6	64	31
Chile	45	41	18	9	14	63	53
Colombia	44	48	14	16	18	51	63
Bolivia	39	46	17	5	24	63	88
Peru	36	43	13	10	20	54	52
Ecuador	21	39	5	11	23	33	71
Venezuela	6	28	2	2	24	12	94

CONCACAF

	Points	Played	Won	Lost	Tied	Goals For	Goals Against
Mexico	114	73	49	16	8	207	52
Costa Rica	81	69	30	21	18	119	74
El Salvador	76	64	32	12	20	102	64
Honduras	73	62	27	19	16	87	67
Canada	64	55	23	18	14	79	65
Haiti	54	52	23	8	21	74	74
USA	50	54	18	14	22	74	99
Trinidad	49	47	18	13	16	69	59
Guatemala	47	53	15	17	21	71	63
Surinam	31	38	11	9	18	58	65
Cuba	26	30	8	10	12	38	44
Netherlands Antilles	25	36	7	11	18	24	76
Jamaica	22	28	8	6	14	27	56
Bermuda	11	14	4	3	7	16	27
Guyana	8	14	3	2	9	13	26
Panama	7	20	2	3	15	13	57
Antigua	5	12	2	1	9	11	37
St. Vincent	5	10	2	1	7	5	32
Puerto Rico	3	10	1	1	8	8	28
Barbados	2	5	1	0	4	4	10
St. Lucia	2	2	1	0	1	2	3
Dominican Republic	1	4	0	1	3	2	9
Grenada	0	2	0	0	2	4	8
Nicaragua	0	2	0	0	2	1	10

ASIA

	Points	Played	Won	Lost	Tied	Goals For	Goals Against
South Korea	96	65	39	18	8	132	42
Iran	56	37	25	6	6	63	27
China PR	54	40	25	4	11	82	28
Kuwait	54	41	24	6	11	82	33
Iraq	51	37	21	9	7	78	37
North Korea	49	41	20	9	12	63	42
Japan	49	47	19	11	17	73	43
Saudi Arabia	40	36	15	10	11	51	39
Hong Kong	36	43	13	10	20	55	73
Syria	35	35	13	9	13	40	41
Qatar	35	31	14	7	10	45	32
Indonesia	32	43	11	10	22	43	77
United Arab Emirates	30	21	12	6	3	40	15
Malaysia	26	27	9	8	10	42	35
Singapore	22	26	9	4	13	32	42
Bahrain	17	20	6	5	9	22	24
Thailand	17	31	7	3	21	30	63
Jordan	14	18	5	4	9	20	29
Bangladesh	10	20	5	0	15	16	47
India	10	14	3	4	7	15	28
Lebanon	8	8	2	4	2	8	9
Oman	8	12	2	4	6	12	16
Yemen	8	8	3	2	3	12	13
Taiwan	5	24	1	3	20	10	92
Macao	4	15	2	0	13	5	70
Vietnam	2	8	1	0	7	4	18
South Vietnam	2	3	1	0	2	1	5
Nepal	1	10	0	1	9	0	39
South Yemen	1	2	0	1	1	4	7
Brunei	0	6	0	0	6	2	29
Palestine	0	2	0	0	2	3	15
North Yemen	0	4	0	0	4	1	17
Sri Lanka	0	8	0	0	8	0	26
Pakistan	0	12	0	0	12	3	48

AFRICA

	Points	Played	Won	Lost	Tied	Goals For	Goals Against
Morocco	72	61	26	20	15	72	46
Nigeria	61	50	23	15	12	82	52
Tunisia	52	48	18	16	14	65	45
Zambia	47	42	20	7	15	72	42
Egypt	46	38	18	10	10	49	34
Algeria	45	36	17	11	8	48	32
Cameroon	41	33	17	7	9	51	31
Ivory Coast	34	28	12	10	6	42	29
Zaire	33	26	14	5	7	41	26
Guinea	28	27	12	4	11	35	30
Ghana	25	25	9	7	9	32	25
Zimbabwe	20	21	7	6	8	16	28
Kenya	19	22	6	7	9	22	33
Sudan	18	20	4	10	6	21	28
Libya	16	14	6	4	4	15	12
Angola	14	17	4	6	7	14	16
Senegal	14	19	5	4	10	16	22
Niger	13	12	5	3	4	10	15
Malawi	13	16	4	5	7	12	17
Ethiopia	13	23	3	7	13	23	41
Liberia	10	12	3	4	5	4	8
Gabon	9	10	4	1	5	12	14
Madagascar	9	8	4	1	3	11	8
Tanzania	7	9	1	5	3	9	11
Burkina Faso	6	6	2	2	2	6	7
Uganda	6	6	3	0	3	6	10

* Player with most goals in a match: Gary Cole (7) August 8, 1981; Australia vs. Fiji, 10–0.

Note: All data updated through 1993.

	Points	Played	Won	Lost	Tied	Goals For	Goals Against
Togo	6	13	2	2	9	7	22
South Africa	5	4	2	1	1	2	4
Congo	4	10	1	2	7	9	17
Sierra Leone	4	10	1	2	7	11	22
Burundi	3	4	1	1	2	2	4
Swaziland	3	3	1	1	1	1	5
Gambia	3	4	1	1	2	4	8
Benin	2	10	1	0	9	4	35
Somalia	2	2	0	2	0	1	1
Lesotho	2	4	0	2	2	3	10
Botswana	1	4	0	1	3	1	9
Mozambique	1	6	0	1	5	6	18
Mauritania	1	2	0	1	1	1	3
Mauritius	1	4	0	1	3	3	10
Namibia	0	4	0	0	4	0	12

EUROPE

	Points	Played	Won	Lost	Tied	Goals For	Goals Against
Czechoslovakia	96	71	40	16	15	144	63
Belgium	95	73	40	15	18	137	81
Holland	91	67	37	17	13	141	58
Yugoslavia	91	66	38	15	13	130	68
France	90	69	40	9	20	146	62
Sweden*	90	67	39	12	16	140	73
Scotland	87	69	37	13	19	125	85
Hungary	85	64	35	15	14	133	74
Spain	84	59	36	12	11	126	50
England	83	56	34	15	7	144	41
Bulgaria	82	71	35	12	24	115	95
Romania	81	64	33	13	18	109	66
Soviet Union	79	52	35	9	8	110	32
Germany	78	44	35	8	1	145	30
Italy	78	49	35	8	6	117	31
Portugal	78	73	31	16	26	107	103
Austria	76	61	30	14	17	15	16
Switzerland	75	70	29	17	24	95	90
Northern Ireland**	70	72	26	18	28	83	88
Republic of Ireland	69	73	26	17	30	96	109
Poland	68	58	29	10	19	105	69
Denmark	58	60	24	10	26	94	91
Norway	57	68	22	13	33	89	117
Greece	55	64	21	13	30	71	115
Wales	53	62	21	11	30	80	84
East Germany	52	47	22	8	17	87	65
Israel	51	62	18	15	29	79	100
Turkey	37	64	15	7	42	61	125
Finland	32	73	12	8	53	62	213
Iceland	24	46	8	8	30	37	115
Albania	13	44	4	5	35	24	97
Russia	12	8	5	2	1	15	4
Latvia	9	15	2	5	8	14	26
Cyprus	9	56	3	3	50	29	184
Lithuania	7	15	2	3	10	11	32
Luxembourg +	6	74	2	2	70	39	258
Malta	6	42	1	4	37	15	128
Saar	3	4	1	1	2	4	8
Estonia	3	14	1	1	12	7	44
San Marino	1	10	0	1	9	2	46
Faeroe Islands	0	10	0	0	10	1	38

* First match played: Sweden vs. Estonia, 6–2, June 11, 1933.　** Player with most matches played: Patrick Jennings (43).　+ Team with most matches played (74).

World Cup Finals Team Records: 1930–1990

	App.	Played	Won	Tied	Lost	Goals For	Goals Against	Goal Diff.	Pts	Pts %
Brazil++	14	66	44	11	11	148	65	83	99	75.00
Germany	12	68	39	15	14	145	90	55	93	68.38
Italy	12	54	31	12	11	89	54	35	74	68.51
Argentina+	10	48	24	9	15	82	59	23	57	59.37
England	9	41	18	12	11	55	38	17	48	58.53
Uruguay‡‡	9	37	15	8	14	61	52	9	38	51.35
Soviet Union	7	31	15	6	10	53	34	19	36	58.06
France*	9	34	15	5	14	71	56	15	35	51.47
Yugoslavia	8	33	14	9	12	55	42	13	35	53.03
Hungary	9	32	15	3	14	87	57	30	33	51.56
Spain	8	32	13	7	12	43	38	5	33	51.56
Poland	5	25	13	5	7	39	29	10	31	62.00
Sweden	8	31	11	6	14	51	52	-1	28	45.16
Czechoslovakia	8	30	11	5	14	44	45	-1	27	45.00
Austria	6	26	12	2	12	40	43	-3	26	50.00
Holland	5	20	8	6	6	35	23	12	22	55.00
Belgium	8	25	7	4	14	33	49	-16	18	36.00
Mexico	9	29	6	6	17	27	64	-37	18	31.03
Chile	6	21	7	3	11	26	32	-6	17	40.47
Scotland	7	20	4	6	10	23	35	-12	14	35.00
Portugal	2	9	6	0	3	19	12	7	12	66.66
Switzerland	6	18	5	2	11	28	44	-16	12	33.33
Northern Ireland**	3	13	3	5	5	13	23	-10	11	42.30
Peru	4	15	4	3	8	19	31	-12	11	36.66
Paraguay	4	11	3	4	4	16	25	-9	10	45.45
Cameroon‡	2	8	3	3	2	8	10	-2	9	56.25
Romania	5	12	3	3	6	16	20	-4	9	37.50
Denmark	1	4	3	0	1	10	6	4	6	75.00
East Germany	1	6	2	2	2	5	5	0	6	50.00
United States	4	10	3	0	7	14	29	-15	6	30.00
Bulgaria	5	16	0	6	10	11	35	-24	6	18 75
Wales	1	5	1	3	1	4	4	0	5	50.00
Morocco	2	7	1	3	3	5	8	-3	5	35.71
Algeria	2	6	2	1	3	6	10	-4	5	41.66
Republic of Ireland	1	5	0	4	1	2	3	-1	4	40.00
Costa Rica	1	4	2	0	2	4	6	-2	4	50.00
Colombia	2	7	1	2	4	9	15	-6	4	28.57
Tunisia	1	3	1	1	1	3	2	1	3	50.00
North Korea	1	4	1	1	2	5	9	-4	3	37.50
Cuba	1	3	1	1	1	5	12	-7	3	50.00
Turkey	1	3	1	0	2	10	11	-1	2	33.33
Honduras	1	3	0	2	1	2	3	-1	2	33.33
Israel	1	3	0	2	1	1	3	-2	2	33.33
Egypt	2	4	0	2	2	3	6	-3	2	12.50
Kuwait	1	3	0	1	2	2	6	-4	1	16.66
Australia	1	3	0	1	2	0	5	-5	1	16.66
Iran	1	3	0	1	2	2	8	-6	1	16.66
South Korea	3	8	0	1	7	5	29	-24	1	6.25
Norway	1	1	0	0	1	1	2	-1	0	0.00
Iraq	1	3	0	0	3	1	4	-3	0	0.00
Canada	1	3	0	0	3	0	5	-5	0	0.00
Dutch East Indies	1	1	0	0	1	0	6	-6	0	0.00
United Arab Emirates	1	3	0	0	3	2	11	-9	0	0.00
New Zealand	1	3	0	0	3	2	12	-10	0	0.00
Haiti	1	3	0	0	3	2	14	-12	0	0.00
Zaire	1	3	0	0	3	0	14	-14	0	0.00
Bolivia	3	3	0	0	3	0	16	-16	0	0.00
El Salvador	1	6	0	0	6	1	22	-21	0	0.00

* First goal scored: Lucien Laurent, July 13, 1930. Top goal scorer in a single final tournament: Just Fontaine (13) 1958.　** Youngest player: Norman Whiteside, first match June 1982, 17 years old.　+ Oldest player: Angel Labruna, last match June 1958, 39 years old.　++ Youngest goal scorer: Pelé, first goal June 1958, 17 years old.　‡ Oldest goal scorer: Roger Milla, last goal June 1990, 38 years old.　‡‡ Player with most goals in a match: Juan Alberto Schiaffino (5) July 2, 1950.

OLYMPIC GAMES (1908–1992)

Year	Gold	Silver	Bronze
1900	GREAT BRITAIN	France	Belgium
1904	CANADA	USA	USA
1908	GREAT BRITAIN	Denmark	Holland
1912	GREAT BRITAIN	Denmark	Holland
1920	BELGIUM	Spain	Holland
1924	URUGUAY	Switzerland	Sweden
1928	URUGUAY	Argentina	Italy
1936	ITALY	Austria	Norway
1948	SWEDEN	Yugoslavia	Denmark
1952	HUNGARY	Yugoslavia	Sweden
1956	USSR	Yugoslavia	Bulgaria
1960	YUGOSLAVIA	Denmark	Hungary
1964	HUNGARY	Czecho-slovakia	East Germany
1968	HUNGARY	Bulgaria	Japan
1972	POLAND	Hungary	USSR and East Germany
1976	EAST GERMANY	Poland	USSR
1980	CZECHO-SLOVAKIA	East Germany	USSR
1984	FRANCE	Brazil	Yugoslavia
1988	USSR	Brazil	West Germany
1992	SPAIN	Poland	Ghana

Most goals scored in a single match: Sophus Nielsen (Den) 1908/10; Gottfried Fuchs (Ger) 1912/10.

Highest attendance: France–Brazil, 2–0, Rose Bowl, Pasadena, CA, 1984, 101,799 people.

THE AFRICAN NATIONS CHAMPIONSHIP (1957–1992)

Year	Winner	Runner-up
1957	EGYPT	Ethiopia
1959	EGYPT	Sudan
1962	ETHIOPIA	Egypt
1963	GHANA	Sudan
1965	GHANA	Tunisia
1968	CONGO KINSHASA	Ghana
1970	SUDAN	Ghana
1972	CONGO PR	Mali*
1974	ZAIRE	Zambia
1976	MOROCCO	Guinea
1978	GHANA	Uganda
1980	NIGERIA	Algeria
1982	GHANA	Libya
1984	CAMEROON	Nigeria
1986	EGYPT	Cameroon
1988	CAMEROON	Nigeria
1990	ALGERIA	Nigeria
1992	IVORY COAST	Ghana

THE ASIAN NATIONS CUP (1956–1992)

Year	Winner	Finalist
1956	SOUTH KOREA	Israel
1960	SOUTH KOREA	Israel
1964	ISRAEL	India
1968	IRAN	Burma
1972	IRAN	South Korea
1976	IRAN	Kuwait
1980	KUWAIT	South Korea
1984	SAUDI ARABIA	China
1988	SAUDI ARABIA	South Korea
1992	JAPAN	Saudi Arabia

CONCACAF NATIONS CHAMPIONSHIP (1941–1991)

Year	Winner	Runner-up
1941	COSTA RICA	El Salvador
1943	EL SALVADOR	Costa Rica
1946	COSTA RICA	Guatemala
1948	COSTA RICA	
1951	PANAMA	
1953	COSTA RICA	
1955	COSTA RICA	
1957	HAITI	Curaçao
1960	COSTA RICA	Netherlands Antilles
1961	COSTA RICA	El Salvador
1963	COSTA RICA	El Salvador
1965	MEXICO	Guatemala
1967	GUATEMALA	Mexico
1969	COSTA RICA	Guatemala
1971	MEXICO	Haiti
1973	HAITI	Trinidad & Tobago
1977	MEXICO	Haiti
1981	HONDURAS	El Salvador
1985	CANADA	Honduras
1989	COSTA RICA	U.S.A.
1991	U.S.A.	Honduras

Note: From 1941 to 1961, championship of CCCF (Confederacion Centroamericano y del Caribe de Fútbol); from 1963, championship of CONCACAF.

THE EUROPEAN NATIONS CHAMPIONSHIP (Henry Delaunay Cup) (1960–1992)

Year	Winner	Finalist
1960	SOVIET UNION	Yugoslavia
1964	SPAIN	Soviet Union
1968	ITALY	Yugoslavia
1972	WEST GERMANY	Soviet Union
1976	CZECHOSLOVAKIA	West Germany
1980	WEST GERMANY	Belgium
1984	FRANCE	Spain
1988	HOLLAND	Soviet Union
1992	DENMARK	Germany

THE SOUTH AMERICAN CHAMPION-SHIP (COPA AMERICA) (1916–1993)

Year	Winner	Runner-up
1916	URUGUAY	Argentina
1917	URUGUAY	Argentina
1919	BRAZIL	Uruguay
1920	URUGUAY	Argentina
1921	ARGENTINA	Brazil
1922	BRAZIL	Paraguay
1923	URUGUAY	Argentina
1924	URUGUAY	Argentina
1925	ARGENTINA	Brazil
1926	URUGUAY	Argentina
1927	ARGENTINA	Uruguay
1929	ARGENTINA	Paraguay
1935	URUGUAY	Argentina
1937	ARGENTINA	Brazil
1939	PERU	Uruguay
1941	ARGENTINA	Uruguay
1942	URUGUAY	Argentina
1945	ARGENTINA	Brazil
1946	ARGENTINA	Brazil
1947	ARGENTINA	Paraguay
1949	BRAZIL	Paraguay
1953	PARAGUAY	Brazil
1955	ARGENTINA	Chile
1956	URUGUAY	Chile
1957	ARGENTINA	Brazil
1959	ARGENTINA	Brazil
1959	URUGUAY	Argentina
1963	BOLIVIA	Paraguay
1967	URUGUAY	Argentina
1975	PERU	Colombia
1979	PARAGUAY	Chile
1983	URUGUAY	Brazil
1987	URUGUAY	Chile
1989	BRAZIL	Uruguay
1991	ARGENTINA	Brazil
1993	ARGENTINA	Mexico

National Records

ARGENTINA

Asociación del Fútbol Argentino, founded 1893

World Cup Finals

1930 Runner-up
1934 First Round
1958 First Round
1962 First Round
1966 Quarter Finals
1974 Second Round
1978 Winner
1982 Second Round
1986 Winner
1990 Runner-up

Olympic Games

1928 Runner-up
1960 First Round
1964 First Round
1988 Quarter Finals

World Cup Matches

Biggest Win ....6–0 vs. Peru 1978
Biggest Defeat.......... 1–6 vs. Czechoslovakia 1958
0–5 vs. Colombia 1993

International Players

Leading Appearances 84
   Diego Armando MARADONA
Leading Goal Scorer 29
   Diego Armando MARADONA
Leading Appearances in World Cup Finals ... 19
   Diego Armando MARADONA (1982–1990)
Leading Goal Scorer in World Cup Finals 7
   Diego Armando MARADONA (1982–1990)

BELGIUM

Royale Belge des Sociétés de Football-Association, founded 1895

World Cup Finals

1930 First Round
1934 First Round
1938 First Round
1954 First Round
1970 First Round
1982 Second Round
1986 Fourth Place
1990 Second Round

Olympic Games

1900 Third Place
1920 Winners
1924 First Round
1928 Quarter Finals

World Cup Matches

Biggest Win .... 8–3 vs. Iceland 1957
Biggest Defeat .... 0–4 vs. Yugoslavia 1969

International Players

Leading Appearances 96
   Jan CEULEMANS
Leading Goal Scorer 30
   Paul VAN HIMST
   Bernard VOORHOOF
Leading Appearance in World Cup Finals 16
   Jan CEULEMANS (1982–1990)
Leading Goal Scorer in World Cup Finals 4
   Jan CEULEMANS (1982–1990)

BOLIVIA

Federación Boliviana de Fútbol, founded 1925

World Cup Finals

1930 First Round
1950 First Round

World Cup Matches

Biggest Win .... 7–0 vs. Venezuela 1993
Biggest Defeat..................... 0–8 vs. Uruguay 1950
0–8 vs. Brazil 1977

International Players

Leading Appearances 45
   Victor Agustin UGARTE
Leading Goal Scorer 16
   Victor Agustin UGARTE
Leading Appearances in World Cup Finals 2
   Mario ALBORTA, Jesus BERMUDEZ, José BUSTAMANTE, Casiano CHAVARRIA, Segundo DURANDAL, René FERNANDEZ, Diógenes LARA, Rafael MENDEZ, Jorge VALDERRAMA (all 1930)

BRAZIL

Confederação Brasileira de Futebol (CBF), founded 1914

World Cup Finals **

1930 First Round
1934 First Round
1938 Third Place
1950 Runner-up
1954 Quarter Finals
1958 Winner
1962 Winner
1966 First Round
1970 Winner
1974 Fourth Place
1978 Third Place
1982 Second Round
1986 Quarter Finals
1990 Second Round

Olympic Games

1952 Quarter Finals
1960 First Round
1964 First Round
1968 First Round
1972 First Round
1976 Fourth Place
1984 Runner-up
1988 Runner-up

World Cup Matches

Biggest Win..............................8–0 vs. Bolivia 1977
Biggest Defeat..................... 2–4 vs. Hungary 1954
0–2 vs. Bolivia 1993

International Players

Leading Appearances..100
   Djalma SANTOS
Leading Goal Scorer 77
   Edson Arantes do Nascimento "PELÉ"
Leading Appearances in World Cup Finals......16
   Jair Ventura Filho "JAIRZINHO"
Leading Goal Scorer in World Cup Finals.......12
   Edson Arantes do Nascimento "PELÉ"

BULGARIA

Bulgarski Futbolen Soyuz, founded 1923

World Cup Finals

1962 First Round

* Congo Kinshasa won in 1968, then the nation changed its name and won again as Zaire in 1974.** Team with most goals scored (148). Team with longest winning streak: 13 matches (1958–1966).

1966 First Round
1970 First Round
1974 First Round
1986 Second Round

Olympic Games

1924 First Round
1952 First Round
1956 Third Place
1960 First Round
1968 Second Place

World Cup Matches

Biggest Win...........................7–0 vs. Norway1957
Biggest Defeat..........0–6 vs. Czechoslovakia1938

International Players

Leading Appearances...................................96
Hristo BONEV
Leading Goal Score................................r47
Hristo BONEV
Leading Appearances in World Cup Finals........8
Georgi ASPARUKHOV (1962–1970)
Leading Goal Scorer in World Cup Finals.........2
Hristo BONEV (1970–1974)

CAMEROON

Fédération Camérounaise de Football, founded 1960

World Cup Finals

1982 First Round
1990 Quarter Finals

Olympic Games

1984 First Round

World Cup Matches

Biggest Win................................6–1 vs. Zaire1981
Biggest Defeat............................0–4 vs. USSR1990

International Players

Leading Appearances in World Cup Finals........8
Roger MILLA (1982–1990)
Thomas N'KONO (1982–1990)
Leading Goal Scorer in World Cup Finals.........4
Roger MILLA (1982–1990)

COLOMBIA

Federación Colombiana de Fútbol, founded 1924

World Cup Finals

1962 First Round
1990 Second Round

Olympic Games

1968 First Round
1972 First Round
1980 First Round
1992 First Round

World Cup Matches

Biggest Win.........................5–0 vs. Argentina1993
Biggest Defeat...........................0–6 vs. Brazil1977

International Players

Leading Appearances...................................41
Willington ORTIZ
Leading Goal Scorer...................................43
Ricardo CARECA
Leading Appearances in World Cup Finals4
Leonel ALVAREZ, Léon ARANGO, Andrés ESCOBAR, Gilardo GOMEZ, Luis HER-RERA, José HIGUITA, Gabriel Gomez JARAMILLO, Luis Carlos PEREA, Freddy RINCON, Carlos VALDERRAMA (all 1990)
Leading Goal Scorer in World Cup Finals.........2
Bernardo REDIN Valverde (1990)

GERMANY (AND WEST GERMANY)

Deutscher Fußball-Bund, founded 1900

World Cup Finals *

1934 Third Place
1938 First Round
1954 Winner
1958 Fourth Place
1962 Quarter Finals
1966 Runner-up
1970 Third Place
1974 Winner
1978 Second Round
1982 Runner-up
1986 Second Place
1990 Winner

Olympic Games

1912 Preliminary Round
1928 Quarter Finals
1932 Quarter Finals
1952 Fourth Place
1956 Preliminary Round
1972 Second Round
1984 Quarter Finals
1988 Third Place

World Cup Matches

Biggest Win ....12–0 vs. Cyprus1969
Biggest Defeat.....................3–8 vs. Hungary1954

International Players

Leading Appearances...................................108
Lothar MATTHÄUS
Leading Goal Scorer...................................68
Gerhard MÜLLER
Leading Appearances in World Cup Finals......21
Uwe SEELER (1958–1970)
Leading Goal Scorer in World Cup Finals.......14
Gerhard MÜLLER (1970–1974)

GREECE

Elliki Podosfairiki Omospondia, founded 1926

Olympic Games

1920 First Round
1952 Preliminary Round

World Cup Matches

Biggest Win ....4–1 vs. Switzerland1969
Biggest Defeat....................1–11 vs. Hungary1938

International Players

Leading Appearances...................................73
Nikos ANASTOPOULOS
Leading Goal Scorer...................................29
Nikos ANASTOPOULOS

HOLLAND

Koninklijke Nederlandsche Voetbalbond, founded 1889

World Cup Finals

1934 First Round
1938 First Round
1974 Runner-up
1978 Runner-up
1990 Second Round

Olympic Games

1908 Third Place
1912 Third Place
1920 Fourth Place
1924 Fourth Place
1928 First Round

1948 First Round
1952 Preliminary Round

World Cup Matches

Biggest Win...........................9–0 vs. Norway1972
Biggest Defeat.........0–3 vs. Czechoslovakia1938
0–3 vs. Hungary1961

International Players

Leading Appearances...................................83
Ruudolf KROL
Leading Goal Scorer...................................35
Faas WILKES
Leading Appearances in World Cup Finals......14
Willem JANSEN (1974–1978)
Ruudolf KROL (1974–1978)
Johannes REP (1974–1978)
Leading Goal Scorer in World Cup Finals.........6
Rob RENSENBRINK (1974–1978)

REPUBLIC OF IRELAND

The Football Association of Ireland, founded 1921

World Cup Finals

1990 Quarter Finals

Olympic Games

1924 Quarter Finals
1948 Preliminary Round

World Cup Matches

Biggest Win ....6–0 vs. Cyprus1980
Biggest Defeat..........1–7 vs. Czechoslovakia1961

International Players

Leading Appearances...................................72
William "Liam" BRADY
Leading Goal Scorer...................................20
Frank STAPLETON
Leading Appearances in World Cup Finals........4
Pat BONNER, Raymond HOUGHTON, Paul McGRATH, Kevin MORAN, Christopher MORRIS and Andrew TOWNSEND (all 1990)
Leading Goal Scorer in World Cup Finals.........1
Niall QUINN and Kevin SHEEDY (1990)

ITALY

Federazione Italiana Giuoco Calcio, founded 1898

World Cup Finals **

1934 Winner
1938 Winner
1950 First Round
1954 First Round
1962 First Round
1966 First Round
1970 Runner-up
1974 First Round
1978 Fourth Place
1982 Winner
1986 Second Round
1990 Third Place

Olympic Games

1912 Preliminary Round
1920 Quarter Finals
1924 Quarter Finals
1928 Third Place
1936 Winner
1948 Quarter Finals
1952 First Round
1960 Third Place
1984 Fourth Place

1988 Fourth Place
1992 Quarter Finals

World Cup Matches

Biggest Win................................7–1 vs. USA 1934
6–0 vs. Israel 1961
Biggest Defeat...............1–4 vs. Switzerland 1954
0–3 vs. Portugal 1957
1–4 vs. Brazil 1970

International Players

Leading Appearances...................................112
Dino ZOFF
Leading Goal Scorer...................................35
Luigi RIVA
Leading Appearances in World Cup Finals......18
Gaetano SCIREA (1978–1986)
Antonio CABRINI (1978–1986)
Leading Goal Scorer in World Cup Finals.........9
Paolo ROSSI (1978–1982)

REPUBLIC OF (SOUTH) KOREA

Korea Football Association, founded 1928

World Cup Finals

1954 First Round
1986 First Round
1990 First Round

Olympic Games

1948 Quarter Finals
1964 First Round
1988 First Round

World Cup Matches

Biggest Win................................9–0 vs. Nepal1989
Biggest Defeat..........................0–7 vs. Turkey1954

International Players

Leading Appearances in World Cup Finals........6
Kim JOO-SUNG (1986–1990)
Park KYUNG-HOON (1986–1990)
Leading Goal Scorer in World Cup Finals.........1
Park CHANG-SUN, Huh JUNG-MOO, Choi SOON-HO, Kim JONG-BOO (all 1986); Hwangbo KWAN (1990)

MEXICO

Federación Mexicana de Fútbol Asociación, founded 1927

World Cup Finals

1930 First Round
1950 First Round
1954 First Round
1958 First Round
1962 First Round
1966 First Round
1970 Quarter Finals
1978 First Round
1986 Quarter Finals

Olympic Games

1964 First Round
1968 Fourth Place
1972 Second Round
1976 First Round

World Cup Matches

Biggest Win ....11–0 vs. St. Vincent1970
Biggest Defeat..........0–6 vs. West Germany1978

International Players

Leading Appearances..82
Gustavo PEÑA
Leading Goal Scorer...................................33
Enrique BORJA

---

* Team with most matches played (68). All-time most successful goal scorer: Gerhard Müller. Player with most minutes played: Uwe Seeler, 1,980 minutes. ** Team with longest no-goal streak: 5 matches (1990).

Leading Appearances in World Cup Finals......11
  Antonio CARBAJAL (1950–1966)
Leading Goal Scorer in World Cup Finals.........2
  Fernando QUIRARTE (1986)
  Javier Huerta VALDIVIA (1986)

MOROCCO

*Fédération Royale Marocaine de Football,
founded 1955*

World Cup Finals

1970 First Round
1986 Second Round

Olympic Games

1964 First Round
1972 Second Round
1984 First Round

World Cup Matches

Biggest Win...........................5–0 vs. Ethiopia 1992
                          5–0 vs. Benin 1993

International Players

Leading Appearances in World Cup Finals........4
  Abdelaziz BOUDERBALA, Nourredine
  BOUYAHIAOUI, Abdelmajid DOLMY,
  Mostafa EL BIAZ, Abderrazak KHAIRI, Labd
  KHALIFA, Abdelmajide LAMRISS,
  Abdelkarim KRIMAU Merry, Mohammed
  TIMOUMI, Ezaki ZAKI Badou (all 1986)
Leading Goal Scorer in World Cup Finals.........2
  Abderrazak KHAIRI (1986)

NIGERIA

Nigeria Football Association, founded 1945

Olympic Games

1968 First Round
1980 First Round

World Cup Matches

Biggest Win...................6–2 vs. Sierra Leone 1978

NORWAY

Norges Fotballforbund, founded 1902

World Cup Finals

1938 First Round

Olympic Games

1912 First Round
1920 Quarter Finals
1936 Third Place
1952 First Round
1984 First Round

World Cup Matches

Biggest Win...................10–0 vs. San Marino 1992
Biggest Defeat......................0–9 vs. Holland 1972

International Players

Leading Appearances..104
  Thorbjørn SVENSSEN
Leading Goal Scorer 33
  Jørgen JUVE
Leading Appearances in World Cup Finals........1
  Arne BRUSTAD, Knut BRYNILDSON, Nils
  ERIKSEN, Odd FRANTZEN, Kristian HEN-
  RIKSEN, Rolf HOLMBERG, Øvind HOLM-
  SEN, Magnar ISAKSEN, Rolf JOHAN-
  NESEN, Henry JOHANSEN, Reidar KVAM-
  MEN (all 1938)
Leading Goal Scorer in World Cup Finals 1
  Arne BRUSTAD (1938)

ROMANIA

Federatia Romana de Fotbal, founded 1908

World Cup Finals

1930 First Round
1934 First Round
1938 First Round
1970 First Round
1990 Second Round

Olympic Games

1924 First Round
1952 Preliminary Round
1964 Quarter Finals

World Cup Matches

Biggest Win ....9–0 vs. Finland 1973
Biggest Defeat......................0–4 vs. Uruguay 1930

International Players

Leading Appearances................................108
  Ladislau BÖLÖNI
Leading Goal Scorer................................30
  Iuliu BODOLA
Leading Appearances in World Cup Finals........4
  Rudolf BüRGER, Nicolae COVACI and
  Ladislau RAFFINSKY (1930–1938); Ioan
  ANDONE, Michael KLEIN, Silviu LUNG,
  Gheorghe POPESCU, Mircea REDNIC, Iosif
  ROTARIU and Ioan Avidiu SABAU (1990)
Leading Goal Scorer in World Cup Finals.........3
  Stefan DOBAY (1934–1938)

RUSSIA (SOVIET UNION AND CIS)

Rossiiskij Futbolnyi Soyutz, founded 1912

World Cup Finals

1958 Quarter Finals
1962 Quarter Finals
1966 Fourth Place
1970 Quarter Finals
1982 Second Round
1986 Second Round
1990 First Round

Olympic Games

1952 First Round
1956 Winner
1972 Third Place
1976 Third Place
1980 Third Place
1988 Winner

World Cup Matches

Biggest Win ....10–0 vs. Finland 1957
Biggest Defeat...........................0–2 vs. Brazil 1958
                          2–4 vs. Denmark 1985
                          0–2 vs. Romania 1990
                          0–2 vs. Argentina 1990

International Players

Leading Appearances...109
  Oleg BLOKHIN
Leading Goal Scorer 39
  Oleg BLOKHIN
Leading Appearances in World Cup Finals......13
  Lev Ivanovich YASHIN (1958–1966)
Leading Goal Scorer in World Cup Finals.........5
  Valentin Kotzmitz IVANOV (1958–1962)

SAUDI ARABIA

*Saudi Arabian Football Federation,
founded 1959*

Olympic Games

1984 First Round

World Cup Matches

Biggest Win...............................8–0 vs. Macao 1993

SPAIN

*Real Federacion Española de Fútbol,
founded 1913*

World Cup Finals

1934 Quarter Finals
1950 Fourth Place
1962 First Round
1966 First Round
1978 First Round
1982 Second Round
1986 Quarter Finals
1990 Second Round

Olympic Games

1920 Third Place
1924 Preliminary Round
1928 Quarter Finals
1968 Quarter Finals
1976 First Round
1980 First Round
1992 Winner

World Cup Matches

Biggest Win ....9–0 vs. Portugal 1934
Biggest Defeat.........................1–6 vs. Brazil 1950

International Players

Leading Appearances................................83
  J. Andoni ZUBIZARRETA
Leading Goal Scorer................................26
  Emilio BUTRAGUEÑO
Leading Appearances in World Cup Finals......10
  José Antonio CAMACHO (1982–1986)
Leading Goal Scorer in World Cup Finals 5
  Emilio BUTRAGUEÑO (1986–1990)

SWEDEN

Svenska Fotbollförbundet, founded 1904

World Cup Finals

1934 Quarter Finals
1938 Fourth Place
1950 Third Place
1958 Runner-up
1970 First Round
1974 Second Round
1978 First Round
1990 First Round

Olympic Games

1908 Fourth Place
1912 Preliminary Round
1920 Quarter Finals
1924 Third Place
1936 First Round
1948 Winner
1952 Third Place
1988 Quarter Finals
1992 Quarter Finals

World Cup Matches

Biggest Win...............................8–0 vs. Cuba 1938
Biggest Defeat...........................1–7 vs. Brazil 1950

International Players

Leading Appearances......................................115
  Björn NORDQVIST
Leading Goal Scorer..............................49
  Sven RYDELL
Leading Appearances in World Cup Finals......11
  Bo Goran LARSSON (1970–1978)
  Karl SVENSSON (1950–1958)

Leading Goal Scorer in World Cup Finals.........4
  Ralf EDSTRÖM (1974–1978)
  Kurt HAMRIN (1958)
  Sven JONASSON (1934–1938)
  Agne SIMONSSON (1958)
  Gustav WETTERSTRÖM (1938)

SWITZERLAND

*Schweizerischer Fussballverband,
founded 1895*

World Cup Finals

1934 Quarter Finals
1938 Quarter Finals
1950 First Round
1954 Quarter Finals
1962 First Round
1966 First Round

Olympic Games

1924 Runner-up
1928 First Round

World Cup Matches

Biggest Win ....6–0 vs. Estonia 1992
Biggest Defeat...................0–5 vs. Germany 1966

International Players

Leading Appearances..117
  Heinz HERMANN
Leading Goal Scorer................................32
  Max ABEGGLEN
Leading Appearances in World Cup Finals........8
  Charles ANTENEN (1950–1962)
Leading Goal Scorer in World Cup Finals.........5
  Josef HÜGI (1954)

UNITED STATES

*United States Soccer Federation,
founded 1913*

World Cup Finals

1930 Third Place
1934 First Round
1950 First Round
1990 First Round

Olympic Games

1904 Second and Third Place
1924 First Round
1928 First Round
1936 First Round
1948 First Round
1952 First Round
1956 First Round
1972 First Round
1984 First Round
1988 First Round

World Cup Matches

Biggest Win ....6–2 vs. Bermuda 1968
Biggest Defeat............................1–7 vs. Italy 1934
                          0–6 vs. Mexico 1949
                          0–6 vs. Mexico 1957

International Players

Leading Appearances..76
  Bruce MURRAY
Leading Goal Scorer...................................17
  Bruce MURRAY
Leading Appearances in World Cup Finals........5
  Thomas FLORIE (1930–1934)
  William GONSALVEZ (1930–1934)
  George MOORHOUSE (1930–1934)
Leading Goal Scorer in World Cup Finals.........4
  Thomas FLORIE (1930–1934)

1994 FIFA World Cup USA Final Competition Game Schedule

	GROUP A United States Switzerland Colombia Romania	GROUP B Brazil Russia Cameroon Sweden	GROUP C Germany Bolivia Spain South Korea	GROUP D Argentina Greece Nigeria Bulgaria	GROUP E Italy Rep. Ireland Norway Mexico	GROUP F Belgium Morocco Netherlands Saudi Arabia
JUNE 17–20	Colombia–Romania June 18/Los Angeles USA–Switzerland June 18/Detroit	Cameroon–Sweden June 19/Los Angeles Brazil–Russia June 20/San Francisco	Germany–Bolivia June 17/Chicago Spain–S. Korea June 17/Dallas		Italy–Ireland June 18/NY/NJ Norway–Mexico June 19/DC	Belgium–Morocco June 19/Orlando Netherlands–Saudi June 20/DC
JUNE 21–24	USA–Colombia June 22/Los Angeles Romania–Switzerland June 22/Detroit	Sweden–Russia June 24/Detroit Brazil–Cameroon June 24/San Francisco	Germany–Spain June 21/Chicago S. Korea–Bolivia June 23/Boston	Argentina–Greece June 21/Boston Nigeria–Bulgaria June 21/Dallas	Italy–Norway June 23/NY/NJ Mexico–Ireland June 24/Orlando	
JUNE 25–27	USA–Romania June 26/Los Angeles Switzerland–Colombia June 26/San Francisco		Bolivia–Spain June 27/Chicago Germany–S. Korea June 27/Dallas	Argentina–Nigeria June 25/Boston Bulgaria–Greece June 26/Chicago		Saudi–Morocco June 25/NY/NJ Belgium–Netherlands June 25/Orlando
JUNE 28–30		Russia–Cameroon June 28/San Francisco Brazil–Sweden June 28/Detroit		Greece–Nigeria June 30/Boston Argentina–Bulgaria June 30/Dallas	Ireland–Norway June 28/NY/NJ Italy–Mexico June 28/DC	Morocco–Netherlands June 29/Orlando Belgium–Saudi June 29/DC

ROUND OF 16				**QUARTER FINALS**	
JULY 2 1C–3ABF Chicago 2C–2A DC	**JULY 3** 1A–3CDE Los Angeles 2F–2B Dallas	**JULY 4** 1B–3ACD San Francisco 1F–2E Orlando	**JULY 5** 1D–3BEF Boston 1E–2D NY/NJ	**JULY 9** W5–W6 Boston W7–W8 Dallas	**JULY 10** W1–W2 San Francisco W3–W4 NY/NJ

SEMIFINALS		**THIRD AND FOURTH PLACES**	**FINAL**
JULY 13 WA–WD Los Angeles	WB–WC NY/NJ	**JULY 16** LA-D–LB-C Los Angeles	**JULY 17** WA-D–WB-C Los Angeles

Official Sponsors

Canon · Coca-Cola · Energizer · FUJIFILM · General Motors · Gillette · JVC · MasterCard · McDonald's · PHILIPS · SNICKERS

Marketing Partners

adidas · American Airlines · Budweiser · EDS Information Technology Services · ITT Sheraton · Sprint · Sun microsystems · UPPER DECK TRADING CARDS